C0-DKL-919
3 2711 00107 7282

Selected Writings of Max Reger

Edited and translated by

CHRISTOPHER ANDERSON

Routledge is an imprint of the
Taylor & Francis Group, an informa business

Published in 2006 by
Routledge
Taylor & Francis Group
270 Madison Avenue
New York, NY 10016

Published in Great Britain by
Routledge
Taylor & Francis Group
2 Park Square
Milton Park, Abingdon
Oxon OX14 4RN

Printed in the United States of America on acid-free paper
10 9 8 7 6 5 4 3 2 1

International Standard Book Number-10: 0-415-97382-1 (Hardcover)
International Standard Book Number-13: 978-0-415-97382-3 (Hardcover)
Library of Congress Card Number 2005032853

Library of Congress Cataloging-in-Publication Data

Reger, Max, 1873-1916.
[Essays. English. Selections]
Selected writings of Max Reger / edited and translated by Christopher Anderson.
p. cm.
Translated from German.
Includes bibliographical references (p.) and index.
ISBN 0-415-97382-1 (hb)
1. Reger, Max, 1873-1916. 2. Music--History and criticism. I. Anderson, Christopher, 1966 July 13- II. Title.

ML410.R25A25 2006
780--dc22 2005032853

Taylor & Francis Group
is the Academic Division of Informa plc.

Visit the Taylor & Francis Web site at
http://www.taylorandfrancis.com

and the Routledge Web site at
http://www.routledge-ny.com

For Lisa

Contents

Preface

When as a student I first became fascinated with Max Reger, I remember that I asked myself not only what sort of music this was, but also what sort of person under what sort of circumstances could produce this sort of music. Eventually, I found out that my question did not have an easy or straightforward answer, and that, perhaps for this reason, it was not often asked, at least not in the whitewashed corridors of mainstream English-speaking musicology, which (I also found out in the course of my education) did not like messy questions and was busy about other agendas into which Reger decidedly did not fit (early music performance, feminism, the state of music in Bali). He was one of those composers who got ignored or — actually worse — got pointed out as a musical aberrant who had taken a dead-end path where the Schoenbergs and the Bartóks of the world had struck out on new and productive ones. Reger was more tragic than other lesser lights like the Herzogenbergs and the Rheinbergers, because — so the story went in summary — these latter composers had produced merely less durable music in the language of their time, whereas Reger had tried to ride on the side of progressivism but had failed to do anything important. Musical Calvinists who preached restraint and economy as both the telos and the virtue of twentieth-century music, a music which experienced its Hegelian *Aufhebung* in (depending on the camp) the ascetic, clean lines of Webern or the so-called neoclassicism of Stravinsky — these voices would admonish that Reger was an example of what could happen when one capitulated to excess and epigonism, a manifestation of Germanic hubris, the end of the blind alley down which Wilhelminian optimism had led. As a mannerist, Reger was not even to late Romanticism really quite what Gesualdo had been to the late Renaissance, since the latter fell *tout court* under the benevolent protectorate of the early music movement.

To my mind, the situation was not helped much by observations like that of Albert Schweitzer, according to whom Reger was an essentially unexportable commodity (Schweitzer 1906: 1–2) — Schweitzer was talking particularly about organ music and about France, but to generalize seemed not to do very much violence to the spirit of the comment. I have since become fond of saying that, for many people, Reger's music is written in sometimes impenetrable German, like a musical version of Martin Heidegger, but without, some would say, the substance. But even on the German end of things, I used to wonder aloud how someone with the broad intellect of a Carl Dahlhaus could write a book called *Zwischen Romantik und Moderne* with only a passing (and disapproving) reference to Max Reger (Dahlhaus 1979: 63), who manifestly stood — however problematically — *zwischen Romantik und Moderne.* While still a student, I began to frequent libraries and antiquarian bookshops with the premeditated purpose of inspecting the *R* column in the indices of books from the early twentieth century through to the present day, only to find scarce if any mention of the composer whom Gerald Abraham pithily dismisses, in his 1938 study *A Hundred Years of Music*, as "that unhappy might-have-been" (Abraham 1938: 230).

I had come to Reger first as a player — as an organist, like so many do — and at first, I was quite busy enough figuring out how to navigate the hyperchromatic topography of these scores (agitato e molto espressivo, naturally). When I did pursue hard questions, I asked how

Reger's contemporaries had solved the same problems I was facing. When the rubber really hit the road, so to speak, the objective was to make this music understandable to actual audiences, not to explore the mind of the person who in 1901 had produced a work as deeply disturbing as the *Symphonic Fantasy and Fugue* in D minor op. 57. I had little time to worry meaningfully about why no one else seemed to care much, and I certainly was in no position (I still am not) to proselytize about Reger's position in what we are all told to call the Western canon. Still, the question that had surfaced when I first encountered Reger lurked in the background: What sort of person under what sort of circumstances could produce this sort of music?

As the music became more familiar and the technical problems less time consuming, and in the course of my research into the organ performance tradition that had risen up around one of Reger's central repertories, I began to notice that certain people in fact had cared a great deal, about the composer not only of the organ works but also of the D-minor String Quartet op. 74, of the *Variations and Fugue on a Theme of J. S. Bach* op. 81, of *Psalm 100* op. 106, of the C-minor Violin Sonata op. 139. It turned out that this composer had kicked up a lot of musical dust during his day, and that in so doing he had been no more economical with words than with notes. During my subsequent life with Reger, I had occasion to bump up against a great number of his words, primarily extracted from the voluminous correspondence he maintained with performers, editors, and friends. But there also appeared a modest number of essays and other public statements, many of which had been gathered together from their relatively obscure original publication venues by Karl Hasse in the 1920s (Hasse 1921), and published again in Hermann Wilske's 1995 study called *Max Reger: Zur Rezeption in seiner Zeit*. It was here, reading Reger's words as a companion to his music, that I began to see an answer to the question I had posed at my first encounter with this curious man. If one can at all articulate that answer, it is no less problematical than Reger's works themselves: Man and music remain conflicted, provocative, and acrimonious, painfully caught between a monumental past and a precarious future, brimming with the bile of his time.

The musical community — whatever that is — will never agree about Reger, but a serious conversation about him has begun for the first time in the English-speaking world, and it is in the hope of contributing to that conversation, or at least of facilitating it in some small way, that the present English edition of Reger's public writings is offered. Max Reger was a respected participant in the artistic discourse of his day, and a careful reading of him yields not only a direct perspective on his seemingly indecipherable work — a work that, regardless of likes and dislikes, is unquestionably worth caring about — but also a fresh angle from which to view the sometimes vituperative musical debates of the time, carried on at such high temperatures because of an honest and deep-seated belief that the future of art was at stake. Igor Stravinsky (who was no fan of Reger) once remarked during his lectures at Harvard College that his words functioned as one kind of defense of music, whereas his compositions functioned as another (Stravinsky 1942: 15). This is a remarkably valuable way to view music during an era when composers increasingly felt compelled to talk about what they do, and Reger's words arc no less important in that respect. Like Stravinsky after him, Reger spends less time speaking directly about his own music, and more time trying to show what both words and compositions are attempting to defend, and to defend against. Again, I do not wish to proselytize: I advance this book not to argue about whether Reger's music ought to have won canonical status (particularly when an adequate definition of that term is lacking), but rather to call attention to the fact that he was an active player in a game that mattered very much.

The following points of methodology are worthy of mention:

1. Perhaps the greatest difficulty of the project has been to capture the tone of Reger's writing in the translation. Of course, certain plays on words simply do not translate, and I have drawn attention to instances of these where awareness of them might enhance understanding of the arguments advanced. Overall, though, and more importantly, the writing owes much of its engaging quality to a crudeness of expression joined to an extremely refined wit, and I do not consider myself particularly successful at having retained either of these to the fullest measure in English.

Although his origin in provincial Bavaria was problematical for Reger, at least in his own mind, as he struggled to make a name for himself as a serious composer, he tended nevertheless to capitalize on his image as a gruff Bavarian who spoke the language of the people, a mode of expression far removed from the portentous language of scholarship and criticism. His way of speaking — characterized by the tendency to lapse into needless repetition, to dominate conversation, and to spin out one joke after another — conformed only uncomfortably to the social norms of public and private discourse, so that, in an important sense, Reger's language complements his musical "language": it is not so far-fetched to regard them together as an apologia for the integrity of nonconformity itself. I had set myself the task, then, of translating not only a language, but also the complicated personality that the author makes no apparent attempt to subdue: Objectivity is the last thing of which Reger would wish to be accused. A laudable exercise? Maybe, but in the end hardly possible to realize in a really meaningful way, and I ask the reader's forgiveness for this shortcoming.

2. Related to the problem of translation is the issue of emphasis. Reger drew attention to his points not only by the habitual use of exclamation marks (here retained), but also by frequent and multiple underlining of words. The original published sources, on the other hand, indicate stress variously by italic, bold, or spread type. For the sake of uniformity, I have given all such emphasis in italics. The context is sufficiently unambiguous to distinguish emphasized words from titles of musical and literary works.
3. When it has been necessary to refer to pitch, I have used the designations CC–C–c–c^1–c^2 and so on, where c^1 indicates middle C. In those pieces that address technical aspects of music (essays 1 and 2, as well as the sources that complement their presentation), Reger keeps simply to pitch class, but, for clarity's sake, I have replaced those instances with exact pitches according to the above system. Furthermore, Hugo Riemann's practice of chord designation employs sub- and superscripts, and I have retained these (they appear only in essay 2), because the context makes

clear when a superscript refers to a chord designation instead of to an endnote.

4. In private correspondence and particularly in public essays, Reger regarded writing as a down-to-earth activity, pursued when a concrete need presented itself. Consequently, many of the writings came about as responses to other authors or events, even (in the case of the brief evaluations of J. S. Bach and Richard Strauss given as "essays" 10 and 11) to questionnaires, or *Umfragen*. Where it has proven practical, I have reproduced brief reviews by other authors which Reger's essays address directly, or with which they have a demonstrable and germane connection (for instance, Arthur Smolian's review of the *Beiträge zur Modulationslehre*, to which essay 1 responds; or Margarete Quidde's protest against Isadora Duncan's appearances in Munich, which, according to Karl Hasse, provoked essay 8). Most of these pieces are sufficiently brief to allow their inclusion in the introductory material of the respective essays. The single exception is Hugo Riemann's relatively extended "Degeneration and Regeneration in Music" of 1907, the title of which Reger mimicked in his reply of the same year, when he answered Riemann's points in great detail. Because of the importance of that exchange to the relationship between scholar and composer, I have translated Riemann's piece here as essay 5. Finally and perhaps most obviously, I have not included Reger's 1903 modulation treatise in toto, even though essays 1 and 2 address criticisms raised about that work. First, it is difficult to refer at all to a "translation" of the *Beiträge*, since the book is made up almost wholly of brief musical examples in four parts, accompanied by cursory chordal analysis. The very form of that work, which eschews words in favor of demonstration, betrays Reger's reluctance to identify himself with the "rulebooks" of academia. Second, unlike the essays and other writings presented here, Reger's treatise was made available almost immediately in an English edition by John Bernhoff (Reger 1904e). In the introduction to essay 1, I nonetheless have included a new translation of Reger's *Vorbermerkung* to the *Beiträge*, the only prose portion of

the book. Where specific examples from the treatise are discussed by Reger or others, they are reproduced.

The materials presented here do not answer the central question I posed to myself now some years ago. They do take one down the road a bit, though, and I hope they provide English readers with some perspective on a composer who has yet to rise much above the level of a curiosity.

Christopher Anderson
Grand Forks, North Dakota

ACKNOWLEDGMENTS

Many individuals and institutions have contributed, some of them substantially, to the ease with which this project has been completed. First among them is my wife Lisa, a pianist of "Regerian" leanings, without whose patience and longanimitas on a daily basis, especially during holidays when much of the work was accomplished, this collection would not have seen the light of day. I am likewise indebted to Dr. Jürgen Schaarwächter of the Max Reger Institut/Elsa Reger Stiftung in Karlsruhe, and to Maren Goltz of the Max Reger Archiv (Meininger Museen) in Meiningen, not only for access to the necessary source materials, but also for their counsel and guidance in all matters Regerian. It should be noted, too, that the present work would not have been possible without the Karlsruhe Reger Institute itself, which for several decades has been consistently responsible for making Reger's voluminous correspondence available in exemplary editions. Both Brigitte Geyer, director of the music division of the Leipziger Stadtbibliothek, and Dr. Stephan Hörner of the Gesellschaft für bayerische

Musikgeschichte in Munich were kind to search out sources for me at a great distance, and to grant permission to publish them here. The introductory chapter came about first as a lecture for the Internationale Max Reger Tage at the Anton Bruckner Privatuniversität in Linz during April 2005, and I am grateful to Professor Brett Leighton in Linz for inviting me to speak there on the topic of Reger and the written word, and thereby obliging me to summarize and codify the themes that emerged while preparing Reger's essays. Finally, I must thank the staff of the Chester Fritz Library at the University of North Dakota in Grand Forks for having worked with such consistent kindness and efficiency.

Figures IN.1, 7.1, and 9.1 are reproduced with the kind permission of the Max Reger Institut in Karlsruhe. Figure IN.2 appears by permission of the Musikbibliothek, Stadtbibliothek/Leipzig, and Figure 6.1 by permission of the Meininger Museen, Sammlung Musikgeschichte/Max Reger Archiv.

Introduction

Max Reger and the Written Word

In 1907, as a contribution to the heated conversation about "confusion in music" launched by the Dresden premiere of Richard Strauss's *Salome* over a year earlier, Max Reger submitted a short essay — a so-called Open Letter — to *Die Musik* that addressed the relationship of tradition and innovation in modern music. When the subject turned to his own artistic goals, Reger expressly declined to discuss his own music:

> I alone know what I have striven for, what I have accomplished, and what I have failed to achieve, and this interests the sensation-seeking masses far too little. Whoever wants to know what I want and who I am — that person should examine what I have thus far composed.

> If he is not enlightened by this, if he does not understand it, the fault is not mine!

The point is hardly original; many composers before Reger and after him have not particularly enjoyed talking about what they do. But it seems a good point of departure for some thoughts about the composer's conflicted relationship to the written word, even if his remarks condemn the legitimacy of such an investigation. Reger might well have been horrified that a book, published to the standards of modern musicology, would aim at presenting him as a writer about music. Admittedly, a great number of words are employed here in the name of illumining certain aspects of his person and work — in fact, more than he himself uses in the original writings contained in these pages — and this by way of an academic discipline that he consistently associated with creative bankruptcy and stagnant backwardness, removed from the practical "making" of music that stood, for Reger, at the heart of the matter. But Reger, too, despite his repeated admonitions toward aesthetic rather than historical stances — that is, toward the music itself rather than words about it — produced a massive number of words during his lifetime: thousands of letters and postcards by which the composer, in Susanne Popp's words, "organized his fame" (Popp 2000: 435); reviews of others' music written during the 1890s and early 1900s; an idiosyncratic treatise on modulation; and polemical essays on other composers and on the nature of musical progress. By the time of his death, he undoubtedly had plans to produce many more. Apparently at the suggestion of Siegmund von Hausegger, Reger conceived a study on problems in Brahms's orchestral music, meant as a companion piece to Wagner's essay on Beethoven (Mueller von Asow 1949: 370–71); as Meininger Hofkapellmeister, he had similar plans to publish his suggestions for more "plastic" renderings of classical orchestral works as addenda to the scores appearing with C. F. Peters (ibid., 38). In 1903, and again in 1905, he entertained the idea of writing a textbook on harmony in the wake of his *Beiträge zur Modulationslehre* (letters of 29 June 1903, 2 July 1903, and 19 March 1905 in Müller 1993: 171–73 and 462). Seemingly unable to keep to their proper place, words of strikingly rhetorical import occasionally invade even Reger's scores themselves.

And all of these many words make for rather entertaining reading, as I hope the pieces selected for this volume demonstrate. Reger's writing, like his music, retains a kind of immediacy and unvarnished honesty, an elemental character often associated, not least of all by the composer himself, with his rustic Bavarian roots. Not infrequently, the tone suggests that the author is speaking off the top of his head: One imagines that Max Reger could have said exactly the same thing around a Wurtshaus table over an evening's beer, working himself into the kind of obstreperous harangue that so offended, for example, the Prussian constitution of Karl Straube (1873–1950), who referred disparagingly to the composer's "Rederitis" (letter of 21 February 1909 to Karl Hasse in Gurlitt and Hudemann 1952: 20). Deeply biting cynicism, unbridled yet refined humor, childish tantrums, hasty and often repetitive thinking couched in prolix sentences, seemingly intuitive yet well-considered opinion — all of these elements meet the reader in the most varied alchemies of tone and substance, and, quite aside from entertainment value, one is frequently left with the same uncomfortable impression that some take away from his music — the notion that one has not understood something that is supposed to be important.[1] One searches in vain for an overarching philosophical system. Neither in public nor in private is Reger a systematic thinker. One will not find his spiritual roots in Feuerbach or Schopenhauer as with Wagner, nor in French Romantic literature as with Liszt. He stops short of constructing high-flung and exhaustively argued theories in the style of Schoenberg and Schenker. Through his struggles for recognition and his antagonistic relationship with the establishment in the name of serious art, he presents an image nearly antithetical to the cool head and considered demeanor of Richard Strauss, a composer whose person and position Reger admired fervently, and who consequently puts in frequent appearances over the course of these writings.

But does it follow that Reger is all inspiration and no intellect? History has sometimes found it useful to say so. One of the earliest characterizations of the composer's artistic presence emerges in a formulation of Gustav Robert-Tornow, who in 1907 contrasted him with one of his most effective advocates, the organist Karl Straube: "The Bavarian is a potent genius," maintained Robert-Tornow,

> essentially related to his time only through music and the intimate experiences of youthful years filled with disappointment. The north German [Straube] is a scholarly intelligence, capable of every type of objective and logical thought; he is comprehensively educated.... (Robert-Tornow 1907: 24)

For Robert-Tornow, among Reger's very first biographers, the contrast turns on a certain unspoken alignment of character with region of origin: on the one hand, the instinctive musical genius of the Catholic Bavarian South, "related to his time only through music," and on the other, the considered intellect of the Protestant Prussian North, organized, logical, "comprehensive" in thought. In part because of the significance of the Reger–Straube relationship from an early date, and in part because Reger actively sought an image for himself as "nur-Musiker," the rhetorical antithesis offered by Robert-Tornow has proven very durable. Nevertheless, the simple, clean-cut picture is rarely the most informative one, and when Reger speaks through the medium of words, we are moved to consider whether or not his mind can really be defined against such a clear, if time-honored, distinction between inspiration and intellect, between *sensus* and *ratio*. And the question is no less applicable to his music: It might be fairly said that, for most people, the real paradox of Reger's work lies in the odd impression of an impulsive language articulated through the strictest forms and procedures, an undomesticated garrulousness ("Rederitis," to return to Straube's term) translated into tone and held in check by preestablished forms garnered from the old masters. The former is the property of a hotheaded improviser, the latter of the musical scholar and philologist: again, sensus and ratio lead an uneasy existence, and on this level Reger's use of tones and his use of words most directly reflect each other in the kinds of problems they call up. To be sure, historical opinion has frequently cut the Gordian knot by viewing Reger — words, music, and all — as an intemperate, undisciplined thinker (as Straube tended to do), or, on the other hand, as a mere mathematical *Fugenmeister* whose pen dripped counterpoint in Wagnerian ink: if we follow either of those leads, though, we have failed to enjoy the complexity of the knot, and, in cutting it, we have missed the essential Reger entirely. And even if Robert-Tornow aims at showing Reger's "genius" by profiling it against

Straube's "intelligence," the simplicity of the distinction, however pragmatic, will not hold up under close scrutiny.

It proves useful to consider Reger's writing as a counterpart, or as a foil, to his composing. Between the often illegible, hasty scribbling of his handwriting and the carefully crafted calligraphy of his musical manuscripts exists a dramatic cleft, and Reger himself habitually referred to the effect of the one on the other. Already by 1893, while still under the tutelage of Hugo Riemann, he remarked to his former mentor Adalbert Lindner that "when one is always using the notation pen, one loses the ability to write well" ("so kommt einem das 'Schönschreiben' ganz abhanden"; letter of 21 April 1893 in Popp 2000: 146). Writing — public writing in any case — is the tool of the scholar, whereas musical notation belongs to the practicing musician. Yet when Reger did write for the public, as in the essays contained in this volume, he apparently approached the appearance of his manuscript with the same care he accorded his musical works: Of the essays, only the autograph of "Hugo Wolf's Artistic Legacy" survives (see Figure 7.1), and there, he provided it the same sort of aesthetically pleasing heading common in his music autographs, set off by characteristically large Latin calligraphy, unmistakeably "Regerian." He remarked in a letter to Paul Nikolaus Cossmann, the editor of the new *Süddeutsche Monatshefte* in which the Wolf essay was to appear, "...with me, the draft[2] proceeds really very quickly, but the *purely technical* task of writing so that the typesetter can read the thing is... agonizing" (letter of 3 December 1903 in Müller 1993: 246). Although he would from time to time express that copying music was miserable work as well, the message — that the "nur-Musiker" Reger was a person more suited to writing notes than words — is evident.

In this edition of Reger's writings, admittedly selective, especially when one considers its contents in light of the composer's vast correspondence, I have purposefully set myself the task of examining the published essays and certain other public statements (but not the early reviews, and not the modulation treatise itself) as a more or less unified body of work. Before proceeding, though, it might be well to observe two characteristic instances that properly lie outside the material presented in this volume, but that nevertheless resonate with it. The first concerns an astute letter addressed to Reger by Duke Georg II of Sachsen-Meiningen, in which the duke responds to his Kapellmeister's concern that too much administrative correspondence was damaging his hand. "When one must write a great deal," remarks Georg,

> it is advisable to write no superfluous words — an art that is more difficult than it looks. Our dearly departed [Staats-] minister [Rudolf Freiherr] von Ziller [1832–1912] was magnificent in this respect, and you should model yourself on him. Permit me to say that you have always been the direct opposite of Ziller. This goes so far that even in the very same letter you repeat yourself and, every now and then, introduce at the end of a letter the same sentences that appear at the beginning. This is related to your very admirable wish to be clear: but many words about one and the same subject more nearly ensures that a lack of clarity will arise. You supply the envelope to your letters with too many unneccesary words, which, with the number of letters you write, amounts to a considerable expenditure of energy: every child in Meiningen knows where you live, and nevertheless you write on every letter where you are to be found in Meiningen. — With Ziller's economy, you would certainly come out with a third fewer words. I allow myself to make you aware of this point, not in order to be unpleasant, but rather to help you. Words like "huldvoll ect" [sic] and "unterthänig ect" [sic] amount to a great deal in such a lively correspondence as yours, and you may certainly refrain from them. (Letter of 19 April 1913 in Mueller von Asow 1949: 466)

Anyone familiar with even a small sample of Reger's correspondence, particularly in autograph, with its repetition, multiple underscoring of words and phrases, and habitual recourse to exclamation points, will know that Georg's comments are more than justified. Perhaps no one had ever been in as clear a position to observe Reger's writing habits as was Georg, certainly one of the composer's most intensive correspondents during the years 1911 through 1914, when Reger led the famed Meininger Hofkapelle. The duke's greatest insight here is the link between the composer's habits and his highly characteristic wish for clarity, a trait not unrelated to his background as the son of a schoolteacher, and one that governed his whole artistic personality as composer and interpreter — as *Schöpfer* and *Nachschöpfer* — and heavily informed his style of communication generally. The strikingly didactic, even pedantic, approach to rehearsal and performance Reger pursued with the Meininger Hofkapelle, whereby orchestral textures were subjected to a transparent "plasticity" based on analysis,[3] betrays the same stance as does the urgent, expressive quality of Reger's own scores, with their profusion of interpretive markings — and so too does the importunate, persistent character of his writing: a passionate belief that what one has to say is of immeasurable significance, and that one will not be understood without the adamant repetition, punctilious guidance, and considerable effort associated with the pedagogical program of a preparatory schoolteacher. That "considerable effort" is at the very root of Reger's uncontainable work ethic, and he was absolutely incapable of reforming himself along the lines suggested by Georg: the style of the correspondence — a kind of alchoholism of the pen — does not change after April 1913. Parallels to this situation appear everywhere in Reger's life. Perhaps the clearest example is the case of the publication history of the Piano Quintet in C minor op. 64, which Henri Hinrichsen accepted for C. F. Peters in 1902 on the condition that the composer "reduce the dynamic indications *at least* by one fourth" (letter of 28 May 1902 in Popp and Shigihara 1995: 68). Reger did not dispute Hinrichsen's charges that his performance indications resulted in an overloaded score, any more than he later would dispute the Duke of Meiningen's observations about his writing style. On the contrary, he agreed to the publisher's conditions in 1902, but, as Susanne Popp and Susanne Shigihara have observed in their edition of the Peters correspondence, the end result presents a picture indistinguishable in this respect from Reger's other works (ibid.). The overt didacticism of Reger's scores could be contained no better than that of his writing, even though their author aimed at a Mozartian transparency of communication in both.

The second characteristic instance worth considering concerns those cases in which the composer seeks to instruct in his scores themselves, opening a channel of communication with the performer through the medium of words. The phenomenon goes quite beyond Reger's so-called *Widmungspolitik*, his systematic practice of using dedications to enhance his position as a composer or to say something important about his stance toward the musical culture (for example, the Violin Sonata in C major op. 72 with its musical ciphers "Schafe [sheep]" and "Affe

[ape]," meant at first to bear the dedication "Den deutschen Kritikern" ("To the German critics"), but eventually tempered to a more vague "An Viele!" ("To many!"; note the exclamation point). Other dedications gesture toward the sociopolitical landscape (for example *Eine Vaterländische Ouvertüre* for orchestra op. 140, dedicated "Dem deutschen Heere!" ("To the German army!"; again note the exclamation point). As Hinrichsen had observed in 1902, Reger's performance markings, habitually entered in red ink during a second stage of composition, contribute to the crowded, busy look of his scores both in autograph and in print. Occasionally, he supplements even this picture with didactic footnotes that aim to convince the performer that some aspect of the work has in fact been deliberately conceived as it appears on the page. This is most obvious in his setting of Sofie Seyboth's text "Die Mutter spricht" in the *Schlichte Weisen* op. 76 no. 28 (see Figure IN.1), where Reger incorporates an unmistakable quotation from Mendelssohn's *Sommernachstraum* (another element in the Mendelssohn reception explored at greater length in essay 9), supplemented by a note: "Hunters of reminiscence motives and similar mongers [Fexen] are reassured [zur Beruhigung mitgeteilt] that this 'quotation' is thoroughly *intentional*."

Now, it is more than clear that no one in 1904 needed to be informed of Mendelssohn's well-known "wedding motive" in op. 76 no. 28, which gets top billing in the song due to its text (a mother warns her daughter against marriage). Rather, behind the somewhat condescending tone of the note lurks its actual motivation: impatience with critical minds who seek ultimate meaning in the surface details of art. By making explicit an intention that is already obvious, Reger suggests that he is speaking to the musically immature minds of his critics.

The notion of intent, or *Absicht,* that surfaces in op. 76 no. 28 is engaged repeatedly in Reger's scores. The organist who plays (or the theorist who analyzes) the fugue of the so-called Inferno *Symphonic Fantasy and Fugue* in D minor op. 57 is told explicitly in a footnote that an entire bar of the principal subject is omitted in the first answer. In the didactic *Four Special Studies for the Left Hand Alone*, presumably from 1901, the composer informs the player that he has "*absichtlich*" ("*intentionally*"; emphasis Reger's) refrained from including fingering, since it is more useful for the player to invent his own. In the Lied "Der verliebte Jäger" op. 76 no. 13, Reger follows a time-honored tradition

— 39 —

Frau LOUISE WOLFF zugeeignet.

Die Mutter spricht.

(Sofie Seyboth)

a) Reminiscenzenjägern und ähnlichen Fexen sei zur Beruhigung mitgeteilt, daß dieses „Citat" durchaus Absicht ist.

Schlichte Weisen. No. 28. Aufführungsrecht vorbehalten!

Verlag von Lauterbach & Kuhn in Leipzig. L. & K. 266 Copyright 1905 by Lauterbach & Kuhn

Figure IN. 1 Max Reger: Lied "Die Mutter spricht" op. 76 no. 28, first edition page 1 (Leipzig: Lauterbach & Kuhn, 1905).

by composing horn calls for the piano; a footnote, schoolmasterlike, nevertheless earnestly (exclamation point, yet again) enjoins the pianist to play "the imitation of the horn … everytime in the accompaniment in as characteristic a manner as possible!" In all these examples, the composer finds it necessary to explain, in words, what the notation is or is not doing: the notes are simply not sufficient to get the point across.

Alongside such commentary, humor is frequently engaged as an open answer to the pedantry of the critics. I have already mentioned the so-called Schafe-Affe sonata op. 72, and the "Fexen" who anxiously wonder about the Mendelssohn quotation in op. 76 no. 28. The idiosyncratic blend of cynicism and humor evident in this latter work emerges most clearly in the whimsical, rhetorically charged "*Ewig dein!*" *Salonstück* for piano (see Figure IN.2), with its opus number 17523 (the "Vielschreiber" Reger), its tempo "Noch schneller als möglich" (the impossibly demanding, unidiomatic Reger), the question mark set after the key signature (the ultrachromatic Reger), and the footnoted admonition, aimed squarely at the critic Carl Krebs, that could only have been conceived by this composer: "I ask that this piece be played backward — so à la 'Krebs'; then it will be substantially more bearable for ears that are 'dissonance-pure and desirous of tonality.'" With the aid of words, music itself becomes criticism of criticism, and the line between word and tone is blurred.[4]

Both these instances — Reger's characteristically urgent, repetitive writing style as pointed out by the Duke of Meiningen, and the incursion of words in the music itself — suggest that Reger never felt his intentions, musical and otherwise, were clear enough, and that those who would encounter his works could not really be trusted to perceive certain details (again, musical or otherwise) on their own. Such an observation is potentially illuminating when approaching Reger's idiosyncratic musical language, and it offers a perspective from which one might arrive at a convincing reading of the accompanying essays as well. Certain parallels between music and words are easily drawn, as with the motu contrario introduced poker-faced in "*Ewig dein!*" That work probably originated in 1907, but in 1904, Reger had already seized on the notion of playing a piece backward for its humor value. In "On April 1" (essay 8), directed against Isadora Duncan's method of adding gesture to the "absolute" music of the classical tradition, a practice he could only view as mere sensationalism at the expense of art, he fabricated a fantastic story in which the Funeral March from Chopin's B-flat minor Sonata op. 35 is performed backward. Such conceptions

Figure IN.2 Max Reger: *"Ewig dein!" (Salonstück)* op. 17523, autograph page 1.

"à la Krebs" reflect the palindromic nature of Reger's own name, and they function on two levels. First, by invoking them, Reger makes fun of the public's degenerate taste, or of the critics' inability to understand his own or any worthwhile music — to such dull ears, the sound is the same backward as forward. In his "anti-analysis" of the op. 113 Piano Quartet, given here as essay 15, he suggests that the tempi of the movements, too, could be done "the other way round — the music will sound terrible in either case." Second, since the crab technique amounts to an arcane contrapuntal device, a highly rationalized and mathematical approach to composition, Reger invokes the attendant overtones of scholarship, only to mock it in a farcical context.

I suggested earlier that the categories of sensus and ratio live an uneasy existence in Reger's art, and so do the opposite tendencies of a serious didacticism and a playfully dismissive attitude through which his humor finds expression. The sophisticated humor evident in the examples cited above resurfaces in the the so-called analyses of his own works that Reger occasionally supplied to *Die Musik*, analyses in which he abandons any serious attempt to explain musical structure in the face of the negative critical reception he assumes a work will meet. The discussion of the String Quartet in D minor op. 74 (essay 12), written in 1904, is descriptive in the standard sense, but most of the analyses are profoundly facetious and utterly useless except with respect to the oblique rhetorical statements they advance. Reger's concentrated explanation of the Piano Quartet in D minor op. 113 (essay 15), offered shortly after the work appeared in the spring of 1910, is typical in tone. There, the composer centers not on the thematic architecture, but rather on what he calls "my penchant for musical discursiveness" and the "extremely bold assertion" of the D-minor tonality, "for which … I can assume no responsibility." Reger confesses his musical crimes to a "revered musical police," and he includes a postscript: "P. S. Should the harmony prove to be not always bacteria-free, I ask all apostles of tonal chastity for forgiveness." The odd humor in this sort of writing derives primarily from its author's having taken an opportunity traditionally set aside for serious, if sometimes brief, explanation in a professional context (in this case, the booklet for the Allgemeiner Deutscher Musikverein's Tonkünstlerfest in Zurich during May 1910) and having treated it with the kind of overt (one is tempted to say reckless) caprice that would suggest disregard for his own public reception.

The association of music with disease in the "P. S." of essay 15 calls to mind a much-discussed tendency of the time to equate musical style with physical health, and it surfaces repeatedly in these writings. In his well-known statement from 1905 about Bach's relevance to the modern age (essay 10), Reger calls the older composer a "remedy" for those who have become "ill" from a "misunderstood Wagner." Reger, whose artistic mission it is to restore "musical health,"[5] often refers frivolously to his music as in some respect dangerous or disease ridden. On Karl Straube's autograph copy of the organ *Fantasy on the Chorale "Alle Menschen müssen sterben"* op. 52 no. 1, composed in the autumn of 1900, Reger had written "In case there should be deaths upon hearing this 'crime,' I will assume the burial fees."[6] Likewise, twice in 1907, he produced essays in which he went as far as to include three crosses at the mention of his own music or of modernity in general. In his extensive reply to Hugo Riemann entitled "Degeneration and Regeneration in Music" (essay 6) he points out that the music of living composers is beginning to appear in concert halls: "[E]ven in the most reactionary cities," writes Reger, "where 20–30 years ago one cried out bitterly if a work of Wagner or Brahms 'strayed' into a program, one programs today Strauss, Mahler, and — ††† Reger." Similarly, in his "Music and Progress" from the same year (essay 3), he speaks of the antagonistic attitude toward "us ††† moderns." Further, he shares with others of his time a tendency to call on pathological metaphors to point out what he regards as dangerous and "unhealthy" to present musical culture. In the essay directed at Riemann, for example, Reger speaks of the "tuburcular pallor [schwindsüchtigen Blässe] of remote theory," and in his 1909 appreciation of Mendelssohn (essay 9) he would prescribe "a thorough bath in Mendelssohn" to young composers who had been led astray by a malpracticed Wagnerian aesthetic.

In the decade between 1904 and 1914, Max Reger produced all of the pieces included in the present volume: eight formal essays or articles, as well as various responses to questionnaires about other composers (J. S. Bach and Richard Strauss), and the mostly cynical analyses of his opp. 74, 81, 86, 106, 113, and 126. As noted above, one searches in vain for systematic thinking in the name of a worked-out philosophical or aesthetic program, but, if one were to identify any sort of universal theme that might justify consideration of the following writings as a coherent body of work, it would have to be their author's constant concern for a correct relationship between tradition and innovation. Whether his writing is motivated by the negative reception of his

Modulationslehre (as it is in essays 1 and 2, "I Request the Floor!" and "More Light" of 1904), by a wish to evaluate past composers (as in essays 7 and 9 of 1904 and 1909, directed at Wolf and Mendelssohn respectively), or by the wide-ranging discussions about "confusion in music" set off by *Salome* and Felix Draeseke (as in essays 3, 4, and 6 of 1907), the question of how the past should interact with the present is writ large. Reger is usually concerned to set up antitheses, all of which articulate and develop to various degrees the oppositions inherent in the dual concepts of tradition and innovation: epigonism and progressivism, the politically informed categories of left and right, the previously mentioned physical categories of sickness and health, and, perhaps most significantly, the antagonistically opposed forces of *Wissenschaft* and creativity, theory and practice. The earnest attempt to reconcile such oppositions reveals Reger's birthright as a child of the modernist age, and these essays present the composer as an important partner in the thoroughly modernist discourses of his time.

I wish to examine more closely Reger's ideas about theory (allied, on a certain level, with the notion of tradition) and practice (similarly allied with the notion of innovation), since they get at the root of all his writings, his ideas about the proper direction of art, and, ultimately, his musical oeuvre. Reger's broad conception of Wissenschaft includes not only the emerging discipline of Musikwissenschaft, but also the complementary fields of theory and analysis, as well as what we today like to call performance (or performing) practice. Under the umbrella of Wissenschaft also fall criticism and aesthetics, and the scholarly and journalistic institutions in and through which these disciplines were pursued. As an essay writer, he was aware that he was contributing to the very fields against which he directed his polemics, and it is in this context — more so, for instance, than in the private correspondence — that his deep-seated mistrust of all things intellectual emerges. In his book-length study of Reger "and his time," now about 15 years old, Rainer Cadenbach located Reger's anti-intellectualism within a larger complex of personality issues arising from what the composer perceived as his inferior social position:

> Alongside the socially privileged ... Reger tended to choose particularly the "intellectuals" as the target of his attacks, whether

> in his composition, in his literary or journalistic occupation, or even in his work in the field of Musikwissenschaft or music theory. Here, Reger's verbal attacks are aimed noticeably often at the "brain" [das "Gehirn"] and his battle cry turns against "degenerierte Gehirnfatzken," against those without ability who suddenly "call themselves doctors" (whereby in his opinion "these days the doctorate in Musikwissenschaft is earned far too easily"), and against the "softening of the brain" of "university music professors," against the "pigs ... whose sorry dog brain dissolves into liquid manure out of irritation and anger," and finally in general against the "aestheticians," in order to be done with whom Reger, in best humor, offered the advice that, if one were to run into such a person, one ought to strike him dead without a second thought. (Cadenbach 1991: 130)

This stance is not merely (passively) disdainful of Wissenschaft. It is downright bellicose, glaringly vituperative, even when considered in the context of the sometimes heated language of its day. Such passion hardly falls from the sky, and we need only look to Reger's most sustained and intimate brush with the ivory tower of Wissenschaft to find its likely source. That encounter played itself out in the early 1890s, during which time he studied at Sondershausen, then at Wiesbaden, with the noted theorist Hugo Riemann (1849–1919). Riemann, over twenty years his pupil's senior, occupied a social position in fact quite removed from Reger's Bavarian provincialism. Impressed with Reger's industry and talent, he had developed a familial closeness to the young man during the first years of Reger's studies, but the relationship deteriorated by the time Riemann left Wiesbaden for Leipzig in 1895. Reger, who had already struggled intensely on both personal and professional levels before 1895, plunged himself into a number of self-destructive years following Riemann's departure, ending in the complete collapse that necessitated a return to his parents' home in 1898. It is clear that he associated the 1890s not only with the positive outcomes of having gained a solid compositional technique and a personal style, both because of and in spite of Riemann's tutelage, but also with extreme professional disappointment and the ultimate ruination of his mental and physical health. All of this, positive and negative, was the result of having traversed the halls of Riemannian Wissenschaft in the first place, and Reger's lifelong conflicted attitude toward theory and scholarship is unavoidably bound up with those years. Not surprisingly, Riemann became the touchstone for the composer's most sustained attack on the errant posture of modern scholarship (essay 6).

In light of the acidic attitude toward Wissenschaft described so vividly by Cadenbach, Reger's activity as an essayist — even as a polemical one concerned with an ideological defense of his own artistic orientation — presents us with a considerable paradox, particularly given that the composer was accused of the same intellectualism he attacked with such acerbity. Twice in 1904, Max Arend, who had been a student with Reger at Wiesbaden during the 1890s, criticized the latter's *Modulationslehre* on the grounds that its avoidance of enharmonicism (as in a modulation from C major to E-sharp minor) amounted merely to an intellectual construct.[7] Such a procedure, claimed Arend, had nothing to do with the purpose of modulation as set out by Gottfried Weber, namely "to force the listener to change his assumed position" (Arend 1903/04a: 79). Instead, the author of the *Beiträge* "pursues a kind of extramusical mathematics of the mind and does harm to the principles of modulation, since the latter must *compel* the listener" (Arend 1903/04b: 112). Arend drew Reger's ire in essay 2, "More Light," the almost militant peroration of which portrays Arend's views as obstructions to progress:

> Although backward-looking tendencies and endeavors, patronized on many sides, proliferate increasingly in music, although especially in music we have at our disposal a vast and imposing series of "Monuments of German Criticism," we — who dedicate ourselves with confidence in the German spirit and open, forward-looking eyes to the further development of our art — nevertheless will not lose hope that some day Goethe's words *"More light!"* will be fulfilled.

Typically, Arend's criticism is aligned with "backward-looking tendencies" and Reger's own aims not only with those of progressive music but also with the "German spirit" itself. The "Monuments of German Criticism," or "Denkmäler deutscher Kritik," alludes unmistakably to the *Denkmäler deutscher Tonkunst*, that icon of Musikwissenschaft that, despite its commitment to making the music of Reger's beloved *alte Meister* accessible, represented the intellectual forces of sophistic positivism and artistic insolvency, here under the leadership of fellow former Riemann pupil Arend. For Reger, scholarship positions itself directly across the trenches from the forces of progress.

In essay 4, Reger's "Open Letter" of 1907, the negative attitude toward scholarship becomes even more pronounced. At the outset, he addresses directly the editor of *Die Musik* who had requested the essay, wondering in print,

> Who should write about music at all? And you naturally reply, "Composers, too, above all!" Oh, no! Composers will always compose, but they will leave the writing about music to the scholars [Schriftgelehrten]. These people no doubt understand this much, much better than do we professional musicians — or we composers — (the ones who indeed "make" music).

Reger claims that the place of scholarship is to write about music, and that "confusion in music" has arisen not from musical works, but from an excess of words about them. The problem is only compounded by the fact that critical writing arrogantly oversteps its authority by seeking to act prescriptively (hence proscriptively as well) rather than merely descriptively: later in the same essay Reger longs for "a plain rule book," one not produced by the prevailing critical wisdom "in which everything that one must *not* do is so clearly and systematically catalogued." Clearly, Reger considered his *Beiträge zur Modulationslehre* of 1903 a model for such a "plain" book. When, during the same year, the idea arose that the composer might undertake a more extensive *Harmonielehre* with the Berlin critic and theory instructor Wilhelm Klatte, he warned that the correct orientation (we would say "methodology" today) of such a study was less obvious than it might first appear:

> Besides … considering the huge expansion in the area of modern harmony, an area that grows larger every day on account of a certain Max Reger, this means an *enormous task*, the scope of which makes me shudder. Further, as arrogant as it may sound, — I alone am the "creative one" [der "Schaffende"] — as far as the harmony text goes, Herr Klatte would have thoroughly to accustom himself to *my* views of harmony! (letter of 2 July 1903 to Carl Lauterbach and Max Kuhn in Müller 1993: 172–73)

Theory follows practice, Wissenschaft must march behind "der Schaffende." It follows, then, that Reger-as-composer viewed himself in a particularly authoritative position to transcend the narrow confines of critical scholarship. And Reger-as-writer, it should be immediately apparent, offers anything but the kind of "objective-scholarly" work that remains the proper purview of the academy, the "Schriftgelehrten."

And that leads us back briefly to the opening passage from essay 4 reproduced above. It is worth noting that the word for those who write about music — "Schriftgelehrten" — is Luther's term for the scribes whose pedantic interpretation of Jewish law proved instrumental in Christ's condemnation and death. And indeed, never far from the surface here is the martyrdom of the visionary composer, like Christ, unrecognized and persecuted in his own time. In essay 6, "Degeneration and Regeneration in Music" (from the same year), Reger refers to "the stake … on which, to the inner delight of all conservatives, I am to be roasted," predicting that "the fire for me will probably be lit from the left as well!" In the "Open Letter," he continues in the same vein, intermingling nationalist, religious, and literary overtones in a colorful and sophisticated style, entirely Reger's own. The great composers are martyred, condemned as "heretics and antichrists," an elect that has "committed grave sins" against the "holy rules" of textbooks. "Evildoers" work against a "critical wisdom" blessed with a cynical quasi-biblical beatitude ("Wie lieblich sind die Schuhe demutsvoller Seelenruhe!") drawn cleverly from Wilhelm Busch's popular illustrated story *Die fromme Helene*. A sleeping "German Michel" makes an appearance as well, in his waking state a symbol of optimistic unity, but in his slumber the image of a *Volk* at odds with itself, subjugated from without. Finally, the nur-Musiker Reger submits to a curriculum in music history led by the resident scholar, "Herr Nazi Lacking-All-Talent" (On Reger's view of the "Nazi" party, see essay 4, especially note 8), active also (typically) as a critic in the fictional German Kleinstadt of Krähwinkl, the civic anthropomorphization of a stifling narrow-mindedness.

Armed with such an ideology, it can hardly be a surprise that Reger from time to time alludes to Wagner's *Meistersinger*, where creativity conditioned by experience triumphs over the critical pedantry of scholarship. The fifteen-year-old Reger's experience of the opera during his first visit to Bayreuth counted as one of the formative events of his life, and, quite apart from its musical innovations, the *Meistersinger*'s message put down deep roots in the young man's psyche. Later, he undoubtedly came to see his own struggles reflected in it together with those of Wagner and other composers "martyred" during and after their lifetimes, not in the least at the hands of the Brahms-*Anhänger* Hugo Riemann. In essay 4, "An Open Letter," he returns to the issue of writing about music by pointing out, yet again, that words are not only useless, but they are also a tool for the voice of intellectual backwardness. "Paper is patient," he writes, "and only too often there are 'willing' pens. — Indeed it is written: 'The marker will be so inclined!' — but often the marker is otherwise inclined!" The familiar words of Wagner's Sachs speak for themselves as a condemnation of the critics: "The marker will be so inclined that neither hatred nor love will cloud the judgment he renders."

Further along the same lines, in the 1904 "Hugo Wolf's Artistic Legacy" (essay 7), Reger dwells heavily on Wolf's (ultimately his own) unjustified sufferings at the hands of the critics. "[I]t would have been much more honorable for the critics," he points out, "if they had brought their own critical impotence to light in a civilized manner, rather than having run about like roosters with a scolding tone as they did in the case of Hugo Wolf." Edited out of the printed version, though, is a significant parenthetical remark: "… that a general shaking of the head would have emerged and even the critic admits that he would have to leave the matter with the honest Kothner's statement ('Yes, I understood nothing of it!'" [… daß sich allgemeines Schütteln des Kopfes erhoben hätte u. auch der Referent bekennt, daß es mit dem Ausspruch des biederen Kothner ('Ja, ich verstand gar nichts daran!') bewenden lassen müßte —]." The sympathetic character of Fritz Kothner, whose modesty and perceptiveness in Act I of the *Meistersinger* cause him to admit ignorance about the construction of Walther's love song, is for Reger the perfect model for the critic, and for scholarship in general. But this is not all: in this case, Reger had pirated the entire reference from a review by Edgar Istel of the first performance of his own "Schafe-Affe" Violin Sonata in C major op. 72 (it will be remembered, "An Viele!"), a work, according to Istel at the close of his assessment for the *Neue Zeitschrift*,

> that occasioned a general "shaking of the head." Even the reviewer acknowledges that, with respect to it, he would have to leave the matter with the honest Kothner's statement ("Yes, I understood nothing of it!") [... die allgemeines "Schütteln des Kopfes" hervorrief. Auch Referent bekennt, es ihr gegenüber mit dem Ausspruch des biederen Kothner ("Ja, ich verstand gar nichts davon") bewenden lassen zu müssen]. (Istel 1903: 609)

This is the proper ethical stance of the critic, and the use of Wagner to demonstrate it proved understandably attractive. But the comment is at least as much about what actually happened to Reger as it is about what ought to have happened to Wolf. Indeed, as will become apparent below, when Reger speaks about other "great" composers in these essays, his tone is transparently self-reflexive: he positions himself squarely as the next martyr at the hands of today's critics and tomorrow's historians, and as such, he is validated as a true artist.

I maintained earlier that there is no place in Reger's work where his distaste for a misdirected and stale Wissenschaft comes more prominently to the foreground than in the momentous 1907 exchange with Hugo Riemann, given here as essays 5 (Riemann) and 6 (Reger). I also suggested reading Reger's anti-intellectual stance in general as a by-product of his experience with Riemann, from whose shadow he from time to time tried explicitly to distance himself. Already in 1903, Reger had used essay 2, "More Light," in part to refute emphatically Max Arend's claim that his modulation treatise was an exercise in Riemannian harmony. In 1907, he launched an unexpected attack (unexpected, that is, from the side of Riemann himself) on Riemann's essay "Degeneration und Regeneration in der Musik" with an article of the same title, in which Reger speaks of the critics as "the patrimonius resident musicology" and reacts to Riemann's assertion that in music there are "limits which ought not be transgressed." Again, he paints the history of musical style as a powerful force that advances in spite of, not because of, "dusty book wisdom" and an antogonistic "remote theory":

> Have not absolutely *all* of our great and immortal figures ruthlessly and with mighty fist advanced into the eternal the limits as understood in their time, that the contemporary aesthetic fixed "paralyzed" in place? (Admittedly very much to the irreparable vexation

> of the guilded intellectuals [again, Schriftgelehrten]! And we living ones, … *we nevertheless do not allow ourselves to be bridled, we will not be muzzled and placed under musicological guardianship!*

Such statements must be very much rooted in Reger's own experience with Riemann, whose theories seem to have repulsed Reger less than did the doctrinaire manner with which his mentor had advanced them. Reger's attack on Wissenschaft peaks in the Riemann essay, and in his writings in toto, when he addresses his former mentor's conception of Johannes Brahms as "the complement to the historicizing endeavors of the musicology that has developed in the last decades." "It would be very sad," retorts Reger, "for the immortality of a Brahms if he owed his status in the first place to his reliance on the old masters, as Riemann believes." Defending Brahms against his devotees, so to speak, Reger tries to show that Wissenschaft has befriended the older composer for all the wrong reasons, and that "musicology only seizes on a great figure once the cool grass has at long last overgrown him."

Death, which of course is the final ingredient of martyrdom, is the portal to recognition, at least in the musical academy. When in 1904, Reger had written essay 7 honoring Hugo Wolf on the first anniversary of the latter's death, he had remarked that such an appraisal was well-timed considering the present influence of Wissenschaft on musical culture: "Their creator has, after all, passed away," Reger writes cynically, "and thereby the chief condition for one's performing, applauding, and celebrating these works is fulfilled." Wolf had been the most recent casualty of a misguided reception, martyred at the stake of contemporary critical pedantry. Perhaps drawing on the overtones of his conservative Catholic upbringing, he often drove the image further yet, making it clear that mistreatment and eventual martyrdom in art is not only unfortunate, but should give rise to a certain adulation among the living not dissimilar to sainthood. Bach, Mozart, Beethoven, Schubert, Schumann, Wagner, Brahms, Bruckner, Wolf: all parade through the Wolf assessment, as they would again in the Riemann polemic of essay 6 in 1907, displaying their battle scars garnered at the malevolent hands of an erstwhile critical sham wisdom. "But hail," cries Reger in essay 6, "hail to those who are 'evaluated' in the same way that the great immortal figures were once evaluated!" The musical temple comprises those figures who have suffered at the hands of intellectual criticism, at the pens of the Schriftgelehrten, the scribes, the Pharisees; in a word, the same elders and Philistines who populated the nefarious critical corner of Schumann's schizoid, make-believe world some half century earlier. The elect either achieved little recognition during their lifetimes, or were forced to struggle against the swelling tide of Wissenschaft. Reger certainly believed himself to be next.

And of course, for him, such treatment, predictable as it was unjust, sinned not only against the precepts of art but against the German spirit as well. In his well-known evaluation of J. S. Bach from 1905 (essay 10), Reger had located Bach's essence in his "proto-Germanic, unyielding" spirit and asserted that the long period during which Bach's genius went unrecognized "is the greatest disgrace for the 'critical wisdom' of the eighteenth and nineteenth centuries." Similarly, when in 1909 he issued his assessment of Mendelssohn under the title "Felix Mendelssohn Bartholdy's *Songs Without Words*" (essay 9), he closed with a flourish, unthinkable in Hitler's so-called *Reich* to come, expressly linking Mendelssohn to the spirit of Germany and, once again, to that of the *Meistersinger* ("Bülow's most basic motto — 'Honor your German masters' — obligates us, too, to honor forever the great, German master Felix Mendelssohn.")

I have referred already to differences between the autograph text of essay 7 and its considerably more domesticated published version. From its example, one might reasonably imagine that all of Reger's essays were similarly toned down before being offered for public consumption. In any case, their author's core purpose has only marginally to do with the specific subject matter addressed and everything to do with the subtexts outlined here, themes that come most directly to the surface in essays 3, 4, and 6, but underlie the discussions of harmony in essays 1 and 2, of historical and contemporary figures in essays 7–11, and of Reger's works in essays 12–16. In his private correspondence, he maintains a noticeably more unvarnished stance when speaking about the purposes of his public writings, in words that come closer to the almost childishly invidious attitude outlined earlier by Rainer Cadenbach. In the wake of criticism directed at his *Beiträge zur Modulationslehre*, for instance, Reger made clear to Karl Straube that his aim in essays 1 and 2 lay quite far from any quasi-objective treatment of theoretical questions:

> Particularly your Leipzig critics are worth salting down and presenting to an astounded future generation, prepared in vinegar and oil opposite an entrée. Apropos: have you read my "I Request the Floor" in no. 2 of the *Neue Zeitschrift für Musik*? Herr A. Smolian does not *want* to answer — that is, he wants grass to grow over the issue — but he will not succeed. I'm going to attack him again, but in a completely different way / as I said: soon will ensue the execution of 2 gentlemen. (Letter of 8 February 1904 in Popp 1986: 50)

The point is hardly to advance a considered argument; Reger often wants not so much to prove a point as he does to pin the opposition to the wall, to "strike him dead without a second thought," to return once again to Cadenbach's formulation.

The availability of an autograph final draft for essay 7 makes possible an instructive comparison with the published version in light of these considerations. The openly vindictive tone of the original was moderated (by the editor? by Reger?) before the essay was released, but the reader who knows Reger can easily peer through the more carefully crafted lines of the final version. The very divergent endings in the two versions of essay 7 reveal not only the extent of polish and streamlining accomplished before publication but also how the author's original intent was to leave the reader with an impression of Wolf as — like Bach in essay 10 — "urgermanisch" and "unbeugsam" in the face of maltreatment. The published essay ends like a tragedy, admonishing the public to atone for "the folly of earlier generations," and asking editors to "listen somewhat more closely to artists with ability, not to the cries of markets." The original conception, by contrast, paints Wolf as a Christ-like figure, "the true high priest of art," subject to the persecution of the masses. Here, Reger expressly associates the older composer with the Germanic spirit and points to "the disconsolate, bitter wounds, all the unspeakable wrongs strewn over the thorny life's path of Hugo Wolf." The lack of recognition accorded his music, suggests this version, stemmed from the same critical blindness that still afflicted the music of Bach, for which Reger offers a specific example:

a Munich performance of Bach's concerto BWV 1043 (certainly as part of Felix Weingartner's Kaim Orchestra concerts) at which hissing was heard. Reger would "ask unconditionally that [this observation] be included as a note," since in his mind Wolf gains credibility by having undergone the same sort of persecution as the very icon of German music, Johann Sebastian Bach. An appreciation of Wolf? Maybe, but in essence a vehicle for a shot across the bow of contemporary (German) musical culture, a culture that held the fate of Reger, too, in its hands.

By way of introduction, I have approached Reger's essays here primarily through the lens of an opposition between theory and practice, Wissenschaft and creativity, ratio and sensus, dead tradition and living innovation. I do not mean to suggest that they do not treat other topics worthy of investigation. Alongside the duality of theory and practice, for instance, runs the nearly equally prominent one within the notion of practice itself, the opposition between what Reger repeatedly calls "the inner experience" ("das innere Erreignis") on the one hand and "ability" ("Können") on the other. When in the fable of essay 8 the composer obliquely derides Isadora Duncan's danced improvisations to classical music, the naïve fools in the cow barn are held in awe by an otherworldly figure "aglow in supernatural brilliance, in whose raised right hand — as if in blessing — was held the Gospel of the 'inner experience.'" The sham of mere inspiration contrasts greatly with the crafted approach to composition Reger advocates in such loaded remarks as the one cited above that concludes the published version of the Wolf essay, where "artists with ability" (Künstler ... die etwas können) should lead. Similarly, his second succinct evaluation of Strauss in essay 11 pays the elder composer the only complement Reger finds necessary for a responsible artist: Strauss is a figure of "the most solid ability — and once more, ability [von solidestem Können — und abermals Können]." This is modernist *Sachlichkeit*, indeed.

Beyond and above these oppositions it is Reger's didacticism — on account of which it was so overwhelmingly important to him to be understood — that informs the tone of his writing, a tone of annoyance and impatience with those persons and institutions who fail to understand what Reger is trying to "teach," and that shuns intellectual approaches to his music and to that of the great composers. In the dialectic between theory and practice, I have suggested above with regard to Riemann that it is not Wissenschaft per se against which Reger actually directs his attacks, but rather its pedantry, its narrow-mindedness, its inability to understand artistic motivations and aesthetic orientations that are absolutely clear to him. "If the efforts of musicology," he writes in essay 6, "are based solely on the motivation of bringing honor to the old masters, then we radical progressives have every reason to greet these efforts with extreme sympathy!" For Reger, however, the ivory tower of Wissenschaft was not "solely" about elevating the old masters to an honorable position, but rather about something in his eyes much more value laden, whereby the accomplishments of great composers were painted in such a way that contemporary innovation (Reger's music, or that of Wolf, or that of Strauss) appeared synonymous with iconoclasm.

As the field broadly understood as Musikwissenschaft looks back at its own relatively short history, and on its roots in the historicist intellectualism of the nineteenth century, it can see an image of itself reflected back in the modernist figure of Max Reger. We need not agree with Reger that words about him and his music are of no consequence. The mere existence of his essays alone challenges that viewpoint, to say nothing of his voluminous, impulsive correspondence. For the reader of the present writings, it is imperative to recognize the thoroughly modernist nature of Reger's own conflicted and urgent efforts to engage theory from the standpoint of practice, scholarly intelligence from the standpoint of creative genius, and — in what follows — music from the standpoint of the written word.

Part I
Defense of the *Beiträge zur Modulationslehre* of 1903

1

I Request the Floor!

Neue Zeitschrift für Musik 71/2 (6 January 1904): 20–21

Introduction

Max Reger's only contribution to music theory, his succinct *Beiträge zur Modulationslehre*, appeared in 1903 with C. F. Kahnt (Reger 1903). Preferring exemplum and imitatio to the byways of academic theoretical discourse, he largely refrains from prose text as such, instead merely supplying one hundred extremely brief four-part musical examples of one or two bars' length, each demonstrating a particular modulation, using as tonal departures the keys of C major, C-sharp major, A minor, C-flat major, D-flat minor, and A-sharp minor, respectively. Each example is supplied with a succinct chordal analysis meant to show the possibilities of common-chord modulation without recourse to enharmonic reinterpretation. The equally brief *Vorbemerkung* is reproduced here:

> The *Beiträge zur Modulationslehre* is directed toward not only professional musicians (theory students, pianists, organists, singers, etc. etc.), but also amateurs, for whom the basic concepts of musical theory are not a book of seven seals.
>
> I emphasize that I have *intentionally* avoided any and all enharmonicism in these *Beiträge zur Modulationslehre*, and in the modulation examples, in order to draw the pupil's attention to musical *logic*. For the same reason, I have given the modulation examples through reinterpretation of the tonic, subdominant, and superdominant to a new tonic, subdominant, and superdominant, that is, so to speak in the form of a cadence. In this way, the basic principle of modulation is rendered the most intelligible to the pupil. By way of the accompanying exact analyses of the modulation examples, the basic principles of modulation will surely be immediately comprehensible to every student, even to those of lesser ability! Of course, all of the modulation examples could be solved in other ways. I doubt, however, that other solutions will always be shorter — so to speak "more quick-witted" ["schlagfertiger"] — than the modulation examples given in these *Beiträge zur Modulationslehre.*
>
> The musician who studies the modulation examples and their analyses under the guidance of an experienced, "forward-looking" instructor, should transpose the examples to as many keys as possible. He should attempt to invent similar modulations himself, and he should perhaps likewise analyze them according to the method I have chosen, whereby his understanding of the principles developed succinctly in these *Beiträge zur Modulationslehre* certainly will present no difficulties for him. Undoubtedly to a great extent, he will be sent on his way to absolute clarity in the consideration and comprehension of even the most complicated modulations, harmony, and counterpoint.
>
> Finally, I ask that my modulation examples be regarded *not* as compositions, rather only as that which they are supposed to be: "dry"

examples for the clarification of the simplest principles of modulation, one of the most important chapters in the whole of musical theory, particularly in view of modern practice.

Should it be granted that my little book might make a substantial contribution to the dispersal of the nearly impenetrable fog that, despite many "inner experiences of the psyche" [trotz der vielen "seelischen und inneren Erlebnisse"],[1] prevails in certain minds, that would be a great comfort to me.

Munich, October 1903
Max Reger

Reger's *Beiträge* attracted the immediate attention of the musical press. Whereas some reviewers, like Otto Taubmann in the *Neue Zeitschrift*, would recommend that the book "should be introduced into every theory course" (Taubmann 1903, 655), other writers received it either cooly or with open censure. In January 1904, and again in March of that year, Reger felt compelled to answer certain critical points that had emerged in reviews of the volume. The subject of the present essay is a relatively brief assessment, apparently by the Leipzig critic Arthur Smolian (1856–1911), in Vienna's *Neue Musikalische Presse* (Smolian 1903).[2] Smolian seeks to draw parallels between the advance of technology in speedy ground travel and the "technology" of "modulatory travel" in music. The article's succinctness allows for its full reproduction here:

Max Reger, Beiträge zur Modulationslehre. Editions: German, French, English, bound at 1.00 Mark. Leipzig, C. F. Kahnt Nachfolger.

The hastiness of modern life, and the disquiet with which the present generation moves from place to place, is reflected in many respects in the newest music. After one contented oneself at first with the simplest modulatory means for getting around, the modulation locomotive of the diminished seventh chord (so called by A. B. Marx) was invented, and, with the help of enharmonic reinterpretation, an electric rail connection was established between the most remote key areas. But one remained bound, so to speak, to the use of the already existing track system, and, after all, this still may have appeared to the uncommonly rushed, unhampered, and high-handed music man of the twentieth century as a restraint, a limitation of his personal freedom. So he invented for himself a kind of modulation automobile, with which he now can race through the wide world of tone as arbitrarily as he pleases. And now there is no longer any calm lingering, no more reflective gazing at the beautiful melodic lines of nature. Instead, the new god of music rushes restlessly over hill and dale in his motorcar, even over beauty itself, murdered by the insane driver of tone. For this generation of high-speed musical travelers, the old doctrines of modulation, which indicate merely the regular postal and rail connections among the various tonal areas, no longer suffice. The need of an orientation map for the world-wandering driver of the musical automobile seems to have emerged, and this need has now been met by Max Reger, himself a mighty high-speed traveler in the harmonic universe, with his above cited *Beiträge zur Modulationslehre.* After a short introduction, the handy little book offers 100 modulations from C major, C-sharp major, A minor, C-flat major, D-flat minor, and A-sharp minor to every imaginable key. Finally, about thirty subsequent pages contain the most thorough analyses of the previous modulation examples. With their precise wording and numbering, these analyses will exercise a positive, instructive effect upon wider circles, although a great number of Reger's modulations are hardly commendable due to their putting beauty at risk through all too abrupt evasive [harmonic] movement. Whoever, for example, can approve of modulations like nos. 6, 19, 27, and 46 in Reger's book, or of the false relation in no. 26, certainly "a new day must have dawned" already for his "spiritual ears" [für dessen "Geister-ohren" muß allerdings tönend schon "ein neuer Tag geboren" sein].[3] We, who hope for a bath of music's rebirth only in a strengthening of melodic sensibility, not from a boundless release of modulatory invention — we can allow the author of these *Beiträge* only the one point of praise that he already assumed for himself in his introductory remarks: that all the modulation problems set forth in the book are in fact solved in "the shortest and most rapid way," to which we then wish to remark additionally that "rapid" musicians, like other rapid people, can become dangerous under certain circumstances.

Although Reger feigned ignorance of Smolian's identity in his polemical retort, he revealed in a letter to Carl Lauterbach, just before the appearance of "I Request the Floor!" that he intended to take Smolian to task:

> Herr Arth. Smolian who, true to his habit of scolding [schimpfen] Reger, has now of course scolded my *Beiträge zur Modulationslehre* as well, has brought out such *incredibly* weak points in his review of the work that I have paid him back most thoroughly in a special essay "I Request the Floor!" … I ask you *most urgently* for *absolute* discretion with everyone concerning the entire Smolian affair. So *Silentium* — please *most urgently*; the thing must remain *absolutely secret*, so that Herr Smolian will one day wake up oblivious and be embarrassed to death! (Letter of 30 December 1903 in Müller 1993: 255)

I Request the Floor!

In the *Neue Musikalische Presse* no. 21, pages 377 and 378, there appears a rather lengthy discussion of my little book *Beiträge zur Modulationslehre* (C. F. Kahnt Nachfolger), which compels me to offer publicly a few supplementary remarks. I emphasize that the Herr reviewer concerned is completely unknown to me by name and personality, and that it is absolutely not my purpose to deliver a "counter-review." The opinion of the Herr reviewer about my little book is a matter of indifference to me, after he likens modern harmony and modulation to an automobile gone "crazy," so to speak, and even more so as it has pleased him to dismiss my little book (a work of admittedly modest scope) with a few witticisms about the modern modulation automobile in a discussion that is certainly earnestly meant, but hardly to be taken so. To renounce curtly a theoretical book like my *Beiträge zur Modulationslehre* — based on long-standing, personal experience with theory instruction[4] and on the clearest views with respect to harmony and modulation — has to be wrong, particularly when one considers what a great, absolutely incalculable role that modulation theory plays in instruction, and this especially in view of modern music! Judging from the tone of the discussion described above, it is not important whether a great number of my modulation examples seem to the Herr reviewer "hardly commendable" due to their "putting beauty at risk through all too abrupt evasive movement." All the more so, since, as is well known, it is not at all easy to determine the difference between the "musically beautiful" and the "musically ugly,"[5] and since the *merely relative concept* of the "musically beautiful" changes very, very rapidly from year to year. The reviewer writes: "Whoever, for example, can approve of such modulations as nos. 6, 19, 27, and 46 of Reger's book, or of the false relation in no. 26 — *certainly 'a new day must have dawned' already for his 'spiritual ears.'*" I will not argue with the Herr reviewer about the "abruptness" of my examples nos. 6, 19, 27, and 46; I have absolutely no desire for such an argument. But the example no. 26, which is supposed to contain, in his opinion, such a horrible false relation, appears below:[6]

(from C major to C-sharp minor)

The false relation can only be that between the soprano's d^2 (third quarter) and the tenor's *d-sharp*^{1} (fourth quarter). Now — I admit tremendous astonishment at seeing this nearly antiquated chord progression stigmatized with such regal indignation as a "false relation" in the year 1903 after Christ.

I have shaken my head and asked, and will ask again and again, how anyone can find a false relation here! Whoever has listened to much music, much classical music, will confirm that a chord progression like that in no. 26

appears in classical pieces one after another.

As is well known, a "false relation" is only possible between a major and minor third of the same triad, for example

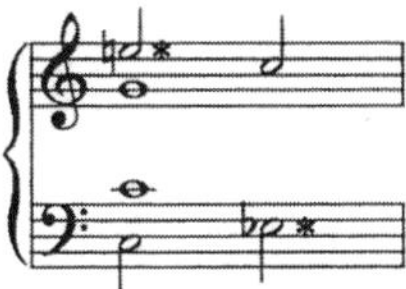

and

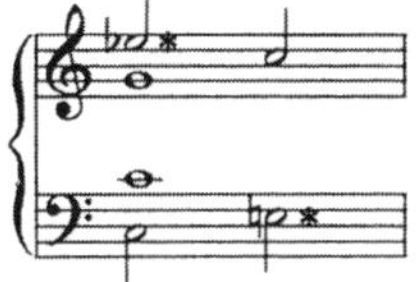

And often enough we find even these chord progressions, that is, the *only* false relations *possible*, in classical works of the masters, even in one of the most prominent works of a master whose compositions no one can accuse of "putting beauty at risk." The relevant passage appears below:

etc.

This "frightful" false relation, which cannot be "phrased away" or otherwise dismissed, comes from the third and fourth bars of the first movement of the F-major Symphony [op. 90] by — Joh. Brahms.

The notion of the false relation is, however, completely mistreated [vollständig deplaziert], employed in an absolutely incorrect way in all those cases in which the chromatic alteration of the same pitch class in another voice does *not* occur *between the major and minor third*. Accordingly, the following progressions are never, ever to be designated as false relations:

And even the progression

(in E minor:)

pointed out with moral indignation by the Herr reviewer, is one long since familiar, common to every student of harmony; it appears countless times in practice. Scarlatti had written it already over 200 years ago, and since then we in fact find this progression of the minor subdominant (with the suspension of the minor sixth before the fifth) to the major superdominant [diese Verbindung der Mollunterdominante (mit dem Vorhalt der kleinen Sexte vor der Quinte) mit der Durober-dominante][7] in the great majority of all masterworks from J. S. Bach through R. Strauss and Hans Pfitzner. Oh, J. S. Bach, Händel, Haydn, Mozart, Beethoven, Schubert, Schumann, Brahms, Wagner, Bruckner,

Strauss, Pfitzner — oh you poor in spirit [ihr Armen im Geiste],[8] who have composed false relations in your chord progressions, so that all who can approve of such "false relations that put beauty at risk" must have "spiritual ears," for which supernatural ears "a new day" must already have dawned.

From the countless, vast number of appearances of this "false relation" discovered in no. 26 of my modulation examples, I permit myself to submit a few additional examples for the sympathetic guidance of all those who perchance entertain similar views:

(or similarly)

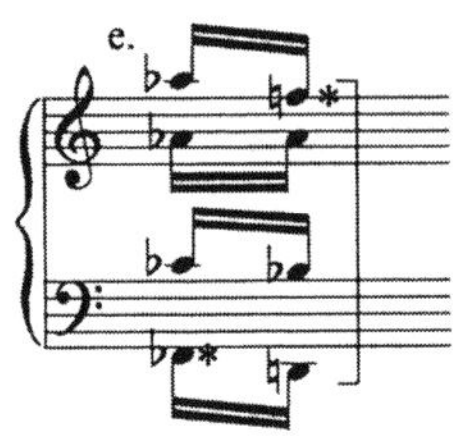

(B-flat major harmony)

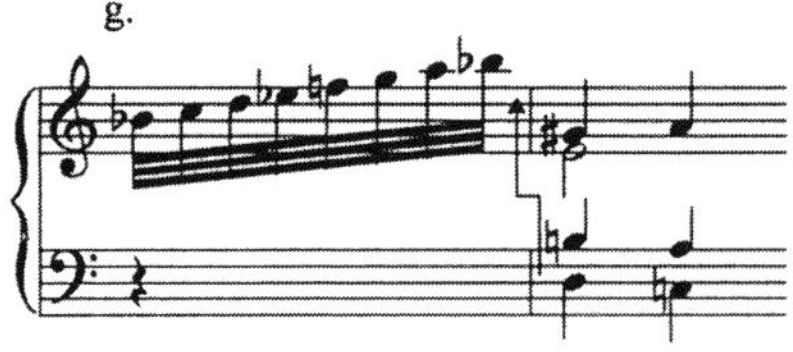

I refrain from citing the works from which I have drawn these examples, of which there are *yet countless* numbers in *classical* music.

Max Reger[9]

2
"More Light"

Neue Zeitschrift für Musik 71/11 (9 March 1904): 202–3

Introduction

Invoking the words Johann Wolfgang von Goethe supposedly uttered at his death, Reger here answers an Artusi-like assessment of his *Beiträge zur Modulationslehre* by Max Arend (Arend 1903–4a), thereby extending the defense of his treatise begun in the *Neue Zeitschrift* on 6 January of the same year (see essay 1). Arend (1873–1944), whom Hugo Riemann cites in 1905 as having gained notice "through theoretical and critical works" (Riemann 1905: 46), was an exact contemporary of Reger and had in fact been a fellow student under Riemann at the Wiesbaden Conservatory during the academic year 1892–93. Arend went on to study law at the University of Leipzig, subsequently pursuing law practice in Dresden, then in Cologne. He maintained a presence in musical circles primarily through his efforts to revive interest in the music of Gluck. In 1893, Reger commented unfavorably on Arend's musical ability in a letter to his former mentor Adalbert Lindner:

> Further, I ask that you no longer use the expression "genius." One only needs to leave out the i — and I do not believe in genius, rather only in steady, hard work. I have opportunity to observe young musicians who possess genius; for example Max Arend, who is now here — a fright of Riemann…. (Letter of 15 February 1893 in Popp 2000: 135–36)

In 1937, Arend authored an informative essay, "Max Reger in Wiesbaden 1892/1893" (Arend 1937), which offers a balanced portrait not only of Reger, but also of Riemann, Albert Fuchs, and others. Arend believed Reger to possess a "fundamental musicality [that] allowed him to grasp everything that was necessary at any moment; he could accomplish everything in music as a matter of principle, if not always in fact" (ibid.: 8).

It is perhaps no surprise that Arend's essay omits any mention of the printed 1904 exchange concerning Reger's *Beiträge*. Arend's criticism centers particularly on Reger's example no. 30, a modulation from C major to E-sharp minor, which Arend maintains the ear can only accept as moving to F minor. Arend regards Reger's use of enharmonicism as purely speculative, perhaps demonstrable in theory but unconvincing in practice. He concludes, not altogether negatively, that Reger's work "on account of the reasons discussed, can be of much benefit in the hands of a perceptive teacher — that is, one for whom it is not necessary to accept Reger's analyses uncritically, because he cannot advance them himself — but for the same reasons it is not without question for the autodidact" (Arend 1903–4a: 79).

"More Light"

I regret that a discussion of my little book *Beiträge zur Modulationslehre* (C. F. Kahnt Nachf., Leipzig) appearing in the *Blätter für Haus- und Kirchenmusik* (no. 5, 1904) has demonstrated that the above words of Goethe are by no means out of date even today. This fact is all the more distressing when one sees that in certain minds, terrible confusion still prevails concerning even the simplest conceivable questions of music theory. Herr Max Arend, who reviewed my little book in the above mentioned publication, expresses views in his essay which I cannot help but illuminate somewhat more exactly.

First, I should make Herr A. aware of his "error at the threshold" ["Eingangsirrtum"]. He writes that my little book can be designated as a practicum in the Riemannian theory of modulation and, therefore, as an exercise in Riemannian harmonic theory.[1] I cannot explain how the author arrives at this assertion, which is left unsubstantiated, since (1) in my little book I do not use the Riemannian nomenclature for chord designation: on the contrary, I employ throughout the tried and true system in general use, as do Richter, Helm,[2] etc.; and (2) I designate the minor triad in the same manner as the rest of the musical world (A minor), and *not* as it would be called according to Riemann, "unter-E" (°e).[3] My single and solitary borrowing from Riemann is the concept of (but *not* the designation for) the "Neapolitan sixth" — perhaps also the Dorian sixth. But even these concepts were *not* unknown territory to theorists before Riemann. Tonic, sub- and superdominant, and parallels have likewise long been sufficiently well known, and also the idea of [harmonic] reinterpretation in modulation was certainly known already *before* Riemann. In addition, I must state here emphatically that my little book will be quite *incomprehensible* to those musicians who have practiced theory *exclusively* according to Riemann.

Further, Herr A. has discovered a few "mistakes" (!) in my little book. According to him, for instance, my modulation example (no. 30, from C major to E-sharp minor) is wrong!

He asserts that all the chords of this modulation lie in F minor,[4] and that the example should actually read:

The Herr reviewer has given this typical example as an imitation of my own, possibly to be studied as such, but everyone will see that it contains a mistake which usually leads to a stern reprimand in theory lessons: the augmented second of the tenor e^1–d-flat^1 (from the first to the second chord). But also the contention that my modulation example belongs in F minor is proven by *nothing*. It appears to have escaped Herr A. that it is quite possible to understand the C-major triad in first inversion (that is, the 6-chord e–g–c) immediately as an E-minor triad with a suspension of the minor sixth to the fifth (that is, the chord of the Neapolitan sixth). If, for example

is correct, then

is *likewise correct, straightforwardly comprehensible,* and *absolutely logical.* The reviewer asserts further that, from the tritone movement of C major to F-sharp major, an autonomous harmonic movement in the same direction can*not* follow. He founds this assertion on Riemann's *Syntaxis*, Leipzig 1877.[5] Herr A. will have little luck with me by calling upon Riemann. As much as I esteem Prof. Dr. Riemann, I regret that I cannot in *any* way regard his music-theoretical teachings as binding for me or as infallible, not to mention that his *Syntaxis* had appeared already in 1877. Since then — at that time Wagner was still frequently decried as the "blood enemy" of German art — certain changes formerly thought *impossible* have entered into *very many, many deeply incisive* views. Thus,

I regret to have to state that Herr A., who relies on Riemann's doctrine in his condemnation of my example no. 30, must be on remarkably bad terms with precisely this doctrine, since it otherwise would be *impossible* to discover tritone movement here. According to Riemann's doctrine of the Neapolitan sixth chord, the 6-chord e–g–c in example no. 30

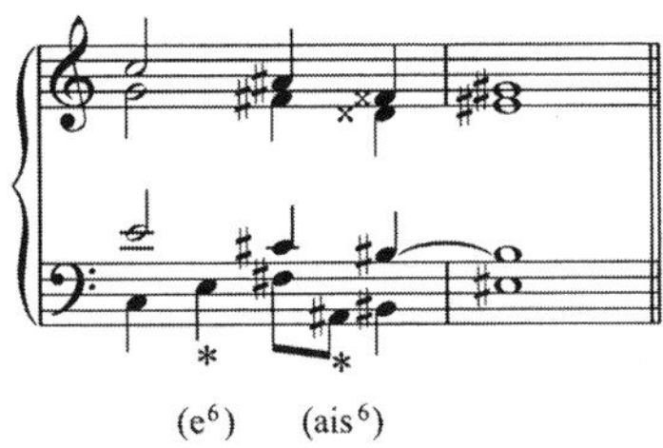

is to be interpreted as "unter-E" (E minor) (°h) with a suspension of the minor contrary second to the primus ($°h^{2>}$), and this °h (E minor) should be interpreted as the minor subdominant of B minor (or B major), which subdominant is followed by the major superdominant F-sharp major of B minor (or B major), which one normally calls a cadence! *Where* is there here a tritone movement? Upon logical investigation, the second tritone movement according to Herr A. (F-sharp major to B-sharp major) is likewise *dis*proven.

The second tritone movement discovered by Herr A. becomes a fable as well by the reinterpretation of the F-sharp major triad's first inversion, the 6-chord a-sharp–c-sharp–f-sharp, to an a-sharp-minor triad with suspension of the minor sixth to the fifth (according to Riemann, $°\text{e-sharp}^{2>}$) moving to the minor subdominant of E-sharp minor, which subdominant is again followed by the major superdominant (B-sharp major from E-sharp minor) — cadence!

Even with the old, admittedly quite simple chord designations, this example becomes clear immediately.

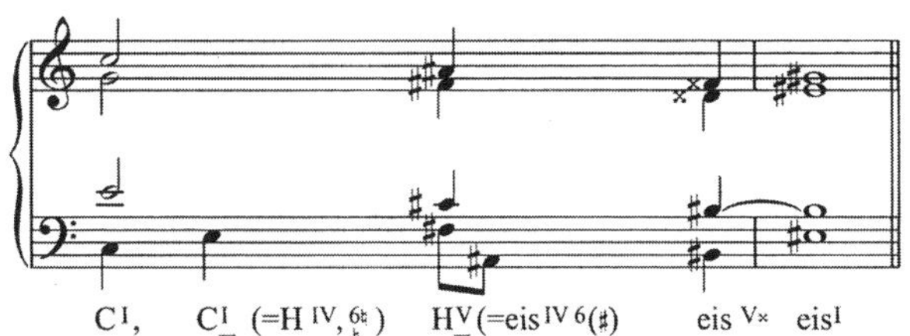

In his review, Herr A. then catalogs a cheerful intermezzo: my little book contains 99, not 100, examples. I state without delay that the reviewer's assertion is *finally* correct. Had he looked somewhat more thoroughly at my little book, then it would have become clear to him that no. 33 resulted from a printing error, which in the meantime was long ago submitted to the publisher for correction in the second printing, already accomplished.[6] As is well known, no prayer protects against the devil of printing errors. This fiend has not allowed Herr A., either, to wander unpunished under the "palm branches of the discovered tritone movements." He writes in one place F major instead of E major and offers the following in his second "typical example":[7]

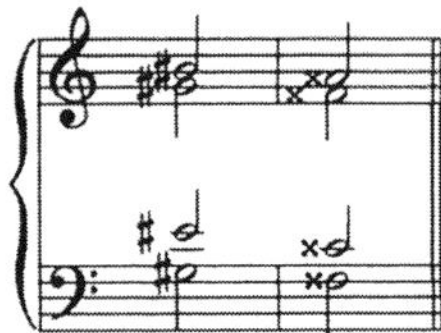

I don't care, furthermore, whether or not Herr A. shares my view that the diminished seventh chord always carries the meaning of the superdominant, since he (as always) fails to supply proof for his view to the contrary. *Likewise*, Herr M. Arend does not justify his assertion that my modulation examples nos. 27 and 41 contain excessively severe writing. It is extremely convenient to make assertions and then withold proof for these assertions. And that Herr A. has paid *more* homage to this convenience in his review of my little book than is perhaps becoming of him, every reader of these lines will now recognize.

Although backward looking tendencies and endeavors, patronized on many sides, proliferate increasingly in music, although especially in music we have at our disposal a vast and imposing series of "Monuments of German Criticism" [eine imposante, unübersehbare Reihe von "Denkmälern deutscher Kritik"][8] we — who dedicate ourselves with confidence in the German spirit and open, forward-looking eyes to the further development of our art — nevertheless will not lose hope that some day Goethe's words *"More light!"* will be fulfilled.[9]

Part II
The "Draeseke Controversy" of 1906

3

Music and Progress

Leipziger Tageblatt 165 (June 16, 1907)

Introduction

"Music and Progress" was to be Reger's first, if brief, contribution to the lively debate that followed in the wake of Richard Strauss's *Salome*, premiered at Dresden on 9 December 1905. On 4 October 1906, the Dresden composer Felix Draeseke (1835–1913) had published "Die Konfusion in der Musik" ("Confusion in Music") in Stuttgart's *Neue Musik-Zeitung*, in which the degeneracy and cacophony of the new music (neither Strauss nor the opera is mentioned expressly) was called polemically into question. Draeseke's article unleashed an argument in print, heated at times, and on 14 June 1907, a short essay by Strauss himself, "Gibt es für die Musik eine Fortschrittspartei?" ("Is There a Progressive Party in Music?") appeared in the new Berlin paper *Der Morgen* (Strauss 1907).[1] Here, Strauss argues that the very notion of a "progressive party" arises from the mistaken idea that the activities "of a narrow group of experts [eines … engeren fachmännischen Kreises]" (Strauss 1907: 13) on behalf of a composer or a style could have any real effect, whereas "the main thing is the compelling contact between the creative genius and the mass of listeners willing to appreciate progress, who far exceed the limits of any possible 'avant-garde [= party]' [Die Hauptsache ist der zwingende Kontakt zwischen dem schaffenden Genie und der über den Rahmen jeder möglichen Partei weit hinausreichenden fortschrittswilligen Masse]" (ibid.: 13–14).

Reger's answer to Strauss was published just two days later. In affirming Strauss's ideas, Reger here attempts to show that the essentially chimerical division between program and absolute music cannot be used to support or debunk the "progressivity" of art. Even though he had become so closely identified with the notion of absolute music in the tradition of Brahms, Reger wishes to point out (as he does again in essays 4 and 6) that he in fact strides alongside Strauss, not against him. In the second half of the article, Reger discusses the dangers of dismissing the past outright, and he argues that true progress can only come from innovation informed by tradition.

Music and Progress

Surely every German musician who does not bow before expressly backward tendencies will have greeted Richard *Strauss's* words, outspoken as they are excellent, with great joy and satisfaction: "Is there a progressive party in music?" Whoever believes at all in the progress and future of our German music and works together to assure this progess will certainly find R. Strauss's stimulating thoughts in this essay to be "liberating" and "enlightening." In particular, every musician and friend of music will greet the fact that R. Strauss — uncontestably the present day's most important composer of program music — himself denies the usefulness of a progressive party. From this we may finally establish that the clique phenomenon, which of late has blossomed so extravagantly, lacks any justification for its existence and in fact is directly harmful to musical progress, since the "clique" undoubtedly is and always will be the "hotbed of mediocrity." Furthermore, what R. Strauss writes concerning the ever-more-noticeable emergence of the "Reactionary Party"[2] deserves the most serious consideration of every musician who is not backward minded. Undeniably, there are still musical institutions — state-supported ones among them — at which music finds an end at Schumann and Brahms.[3] In this respect one can, over time, assemble a delightful collection of quotes from "reputable" instructors at such institutions — a collection of judgments about "modern" music — such that one might run the risk of having to put serious doubt in the intelligence of these gentlemen, if one did not realize that merely plump comfort, intellectual laziness, envy, bitterness at failures suffered, weakness of age, etc. drive this kind of thinking (hostile to modernity, hence adverse to culture as well) about us ††† moderns! A group of critics, whose views about art are rooted in a petrified aesthetic of former times, is working more zealously than ever to make life difficult for those who strive *beyond* this aesthetic. This fact is undeniable, as R. Strauss writes, when one plays the delightful joke of reading critiques of one and the same work performed in various cities![4] Among living musicians, particularly R. Strauss and my humble self have had the honor of experiencing the most humorous things in this respect! Only recently in Berlin did the *monstrous* act come to pass that an artist like R. Strauss, who has long since earned for himself a *place of honor* among composers of all times, was voted upon for membership in the Akademie der Künste and — denied outright:[5] for future generations a fact to be laughed at, and for us living and *striving* artists deeply shameful on account of such a reaction or — — — — — ! Likewise it could occur, just a few weeks ago, that R. Strauss and my poor self were promoted, softly and tenderly, to a "better unmusical hereafter" by the Herren Brandes and Spiro[6] — certainly with a negative result: R. Strauss recuperated in Scheveningen from the exertions of the *Salome* tour, and I am quite well and think — in my altogether honest way — that the world is arranged so that the earth will *never* be depopulated.

One can and must voice agreement with everything that R. Strauss has written in his essay! There is only one sentence that gives me pause for thought. R. Strauss writes: "Away with everything that can produce no other justification for itself than the fact that it already was so yesterday!" ["Fort mit allem, was keine andere Berechtigung für sich aufweisen kann, als daß es gestern schon gewesen ist!"][7] *Of this*, too, *I approve completely*. But since in the midst of the battle of opinions it is not so easy to establish beyond doubt what "was so yesterday," I find this statement of R. Strauss's "dangerous"! We have at present in Germany circles of musicians — I do not need to name these gentlemen — in which J. Brahms is mocked as a long-since superseded affair. And only now, with the newly emerging preference for *chamber music*, for absolute music — after the eternal program music and all its degenerate offshoots have upset the stomach — it has again occured to our dear German what an *endlessly rich treasure of true German art and depth of soul J. Brahms has given the German people*! And Brahms was supposed to have issued from the so-very-distant past! (All indications suggest that Brahms comes from the distant future!)[8] There are the *musical elderly*, too, who of course celebrate Anton Bruckner in theory, but who are proudly indignant should Bruckner be "practically" performed! Maybe Bruckner is also from "yesterday"? That which is "dangerous" about this statement of R. Strauss is that these "musical chauffeurs" — to whom Wagner, G. Mahler, and R. Strauss appear as long-since superseded, discarded great figures from "yesterday" — only now will unfurl the flag of their "progressiveness." Furthermore, perhaps to an even greater degree than earlier, those self-infatuated individuals without the necessary talent and *ability* (the latter unfortunately *too often* lacking)[9] consider their own often tragic creations to be "futuristic." The immediate and distant past in our art cannot be pressed urgently enough upon the hearts of the young who strive with us! And concerning those young individuals who believe that sufficient progress comes when one puts on a red Jacobian cap and cries out "Down with the tyrants!" (the "people from yesterday"): it cannot be made emphatically clear enough to these people that *true* progress can only come and be expected on the basis of the most *exact* and *loving* knowledge of the works of those "from yesterday," that above all progress can only grow out of *ability* — the *kind of ability* which those "from yesterday" possessed always in exemplary ways, bequeathed to us so that we might imitate and emulate it. (See Figure 3.1,

Figure 3.1 Karl Straube: Alte Meister title page, with dedication "To the young master Max Reger" (Edition Peters 3065, 1904).

Karl Straube's rhetorical dedication of his collection "Old Masters" to the "young master" Reger.)

"No master has ever fallen out of the sky," and the history of those masters "from yesterday" is a shining example for us "from today," a bitterly earnest admonition to us "from today" to treat the heritage, the sheer unmistakable heritage passed to us, with *freshness and freedom, full of devotion to the genius of those "from yesterday."* Let us proceed with *prudency, strength, and courage to the honor of those "from yesterday"*![10]

4

An Open Letter

Die Musik 7/1 (October 1907): 10–14

Introduction

Reger's "An Open Letter" in effect continues the argument set out in his "Music and Progress" of some four months earlier. Echoing Strauss's statement in "Is There a Progressive Party in Music?" Reger asserts that much writing about music — including historical assessments, analytical discussions of style, and predictions about future direction — is useless and often issues from those who are unable to judge music armed with anything beyond the pedantic orthodoxy of theory books. In an essay uncommonly rich in religious and political overtones, he denounces the "clique phenomenon" in critical circles of the period, and he again aligns himself with Strauss by announcing that the symphonic poem per se is a legitimate form "so long as it is simply music."[1] Finally, Reger again takes up the notion of "progress" in music, and he points out that true progress cannot reside in the categorical pronouncements of ideological parties (Brahms-Reger versus Wagner-Strauss, for instance). For Reger, art never proceeds from romanticized notions of inspiration, rather from a craftsmanlike ability which, only after a long learning process, may be applied "to break the form with a wise hand, that is, to broaden, to deepen it."

An Open Letter

Dear Editor!

When, a few weeks ago, you invited me to submit a small essay or other such contribution to *Die Musik*, I actually had to shudder! I ask you: I, who all my life has been accustomed to making my way by writing music, who enthusiastically pays homage to the view that, precisely at present, far too many of the non-elect — occasionally also the elect — put pen to paper [geschriftstellert] and also probably plagiarize [geschriftstehlert] — I, then, am supposed to add to the nearly incalculable number of those who through their writings have contributed to the rise of "confusion in music"!! No, you cannot, must not expect or require this of me! — Who should write about music at all? And you naturally reply, "Composers, too, above all!" Oh, no! Composers will always compose, but they will leave the writing about music to the scholars [Schriftgelehrten].[2] These people no doubt understand this much, much better than do we professional musicians — or we composers — (the ones who indeed "make" music). And finally, what should I write about? Our great masters? That would be quite pointless from the start, because whoever today does not yet know who our great masters were and what they have given us by way of eternal example — I cannot teach these "intellectuals" any better; it would be love's labours completely lost [total verlorne Liebesmüh'].[3] Because: Blessed are the poor in spirit! [Selig sind die Armen im Geiste!][4] — Shall I perhaps play the oracle concerning the future of our music in fifty or a hundred years? Spare me! Surely you know that there is nothing more dangerous or nonsensical than prophesying about the future of an art. The future, or if you will, the future present [die zukünftige Gegenwart], will always be represented and led by only a few "heads." Such "contrary persons" were always unpleasant, fatal to and hated by contented mediocrity and patented lazy thinking. Unfortunately every era has had such "wicked fellows" — Apollo, though, will not torment them — they who wanted progress partout, who went their own way without reverent awe before the "great figures of reaction and mediocrity." And observe, dear Editor, it was precisely the great masters who created new and unusual things without ever having considered that they so brutally disturbed the sweet slumber of a highly venerable public and the backwardness of all the antagonistic experts, greying in their eminence and lofty rank. All the brilliant, immortal figures of our art history from Palestrina to the end of this world were and are such "heretics and antichrists"!

This fact is particularly regrettable when one considers what "grave sins" precisely these elect have committed and, it is hoped, will commit until the end of all time! Take any textbook of harmony, counterpoint, etc. etc. — you will see immediately how irreverently these elect have sinned against the "holy" rules of our textbooks! These elect could certainly "create" — even the most fantastic envy and the greatest narrowmindedness must admit this — but to write textbooks in which everything that one must *not* do is so clearly and systematically cataloged, this the elect could not do. Oh, how I long for a plain rule book — one written from the innermost regions of the heart — for music![5] You see, the confusion is great!

Another thing that these elect could never do — and probably will never learn to do — is "to write criticism"!

He who finally makes it clear to himself how countless many times the critics have "missed the mark" and surely will "miss the mark" in the future — only he can measure what an enormous harm this is for the poor "elect" in our view. Here, these "elect" are again the evildoers. Why must they compose just so, that one had to (and still does and always will) "miss the mark"? "How blessed are the shoes of the soul's humble tranquillity!" ["Wie lieblich sind die Schuhe demutsvoller Seelenruhe!"][6] Yes — this humble tranquillity of the soul, this basic requirement for the work of "critical wisdom," this these evildoers never possessed. Full of surging passion and ruthless energy they created work after work, until finally the German Michel woke, growling and yawning, from the sleep into which mediocrity and a reactionary backwardness had hypnotized him.[7]

Should I be mistaken in these matters, dear Editor, I am gladly willing to take a year's instruction in music history under Herr Nazi Lacking-All-Talent [bei Herrn Nazi Ohnallestalent],[8] musical correspondent for the Krähwinkl *Daily News*.[9] In exchange I shall then give him lessons in the basic elements of music (for instance, key, time signature, rhythm, perhaps also intervals), and then — then we both will have benefited! —

Or perhaps do you expect me to offer you a retrospective of my work thus far, after I in my excessive productivity have just completed my op. 100 [*Variations and Fugue on a Theme of Johann Adam Hiller* for orchestra, 1907, dedicated to Fritz Steinbach], to the horror of all those who stand atop the "watchtower of art" [zum Entsetzen aller derer, die auf der "Warte der Kunst" stehen]?[10] That, too, is impossible for me. Apart from the fact that I too much dislike speaking about myself, I think that only such retrospectives of a semiserious kind are justified, such as appear in the *Kladderadatsch* or *Simplizissimus*.[11] These days one looks backward much too much — with much pathos — and for God's sake we ought not become sentimental and pour stale raspberry juice into the intensely fermenting new wine of our time! I alone know for what I have striven, what I have accomplished, and what I have failed to achieve, and this interests the sensation-seeking masses far too little. Whoever wants to know what I want and who I am — that person should examine what I have thus far composed [geschrieben]. If he is not enlightened by this, if he does not understand it, the fault is not mine! I will admit to him in complete confidence that, *before* my op. 1 [Sonata for Violin and Piano in D minor, 1890, dedicated to Hugo Riemann], I was an evil disciple of the symphonic poem. As a 13- to 17-year-old youth, I perpetrated a mass of music, youthful nonsense for which one would need an exact "guide" to make sense of it.[12] Now you will regard me as an archreactionary, or even an apostate or something still worse! But there even you, dear Editor, miss the mark entirely! I am absolutely *not* an enemy of the symphonic poem, and anyone who asserts the opposite pronounces an underhanded lie. If you wish, *every* art work that reveals something of a soul to me is a symphonic poem. I fully acknowledge the justification of the symphonic poem, but I permit myself the right "to be allowed salvation according to my façon" ["nach meiner Façon selig werden zu dürfen"]![13] For me, all music, whether absolute or symphonic poem, is very welcome *so long as it is simply music. But what is music?* It is well known that the Shah of Persia has a different view of this from that of us westerners, and, as you well know, reactionary musicians have in every period thought differently from those who strive forwards. And finally, even in those circles that are sympathetic to the progressive urge, even in those circles that themselves participate in this progress, prevails a wholly different concept of what music is — — — *all according to the respective clique*!!!

This phenomenon of the clique, today so very freshly, devoutly, happily — but not freely — blossoming [frisch, fromm, fröhlich — aber nicht frei — blühende],[14] I regard as one of the greatest backward misfortunes, alongside yet other things, in our artistic life. Of course every person has the right to declare this or that figure among active artists as the sole "Lord God," since every fool likes his own hat the best. But when the clique phenomenon petrifies to such an extent that one opposes, a tout prix and with all possible decent and indecent means, every "productive artist" who even stands at a distance from — to say nothing of adopting a hostile stance toward — the respective clique, then this is a very distressing symptom for "tolerance" — as is well known, the basis of all *un*constrained thinking — among musicians. And precisely in the big German cities like Berlin, Munich, and others, this clique phenomenon is supposed to be in the fullest greenhouse blossom. (Have I been misinformed in this regard??) Thereby is a great deal of damage done. Only one who adopts a removed, objective stance can tell himself with a pleasant, only-too-very-justified grin that such greenhouse blossoms require a great, great deal of — manure [Mist]! — Despite the Allgemeiner Deutscher Musikverein,[15] there is lacking an unqualified "inner solidarity" of all those who, progressive in a *healthy* sense, energetically form a front against all public and "masked" regressives, of whom we have plenty.

But what is *progress*? I admit publicly to you that I am not able to recognize as such everything that this or that clique commends to me as the "only true" progress. Paper is patient, and only too often there are "willing" pens. — Indeed it is written: "The marker will be so inclined!"[16] — but often the marker is *otherwise* inclined! I am likewise unable to acknowledge as the bearers of progress *those* who, in youthful rapture, smile sarcastically at masters like Mendelssohn and Schumann. Oh, what have I already encountered from such "new music composers"! These heroes can turn phrases that make us gape in awe — but I have seen the truth in their works! Furthermore, it is undeniable that in our day, of the many who mount Pegasus, only very few have a grasp of riding. The great and in itself magnificent concept of "inner experience" has had a terrible effect on immature minds. In certain circles one has virtually unlearned that art comes from ability. The misappropriated catchphrase "inner experience" deceives only the fool. One has too often forgotten that, without exception, our masters first absolved a strict program of study, first thoroughly learned the "craftsmanship" of art, before they went on to break the form with a wise hand, that is, to broaden it, to deepen it. Thus our "youngest" have it completely the wrong way round when they think, for instance, that they as Lieder composers must take up where Hugo Wolf left off. One ought not forget what an enormous development Hugo Wolf underwent.[17] The same goes for the imitators of Richard Strauss. What an immeasurably long way it is from Strauss's F-minor Symphony [op. 12, 1884] to *Salome* [op. 54, 1903–5]! Of course, when such absurdities can occur, as a short while ago when a modish musical mind [Musikschöngeist] — but certainly not a "*strong* musical mind" ["Musik*stark*geist"] — described *Salome* as quasi–chamber music, then one cannot be surprised at the most outrageous nonsense. Goethe himself must be amended to "The 'impossible' here is perfected!" ["Das 'Unmögliche,' hier wird's Ereignis!"][18]

On the other hand, you know very well, dear Editor, that unfortunately all too often it is particularly at the state institutions, like the Hochschulen, academies, and conservatories of music, that the most regressive tendencies conceivable are considered infallible.[19] You are aware that even Richard Wagner is today still an uncomfortable figure for certain German professors of musicology, composition, and counterpoint. "In Berlin is said to live a man named Richard Strauss who even calls himself a composer": this statement of a German counterpoint professor is herewith nailed down and preserved for the heartfelt pleasure of future generations.[20] In early 1907 in Berlin, the "wonderful" fact could come to pass that, in his bid for election to membership in the Royal Akademie der Künste, Richard Strauss — was denied. You see, very dear Editor, this is another of those dunce's tales as *only* could drive the German Michel to his breaking point. Yes, yes, the people of thinkers and poets [Ja, ja, das Volk der Denker und Dichter]![21] Do you now know on which side the "confusion in music" has had the worst effect?

In hopes of improvement in this confusion and with the best greetings,

Your most devoted
Max Reger
Colberg a/Ostsee, 5 September 1907

5

Hugo Riemann: Degeneration and Regeneration in Music

Max Hesses Deutscher Musikerkalender 1908: 136–38

Introduction

At the time of his "Degeneration and Regeneration in Music," Hugo Riemann (1849–1919) was at the height of his multifarious career as theorist, historian, aesthetician, lexicographer, editor, teacher, and leader of the University of Leipzig's Collegium musicum. Reger had studied under Riemann in Sondershausen and then Wiesbaden from 1890 through 1895, but the relationship between the two had deteriorated significantly already by 1895, when Riemann accepted a university post in

Leipzig. Essay 5 (by Riemann) and essay 6 (Reger's reply) are pivotal in the history of the relationship, even though Riemann largely restricts his writing to impersonal observations and never mentions Reger.

Arguing somewhat nostalgically from the perspective of history, Riemann observes that an undisciplined and market-driven element in modern musical culture has resulted in very little of worth, and that those works that actually do merit serious attention are set aside in favor of trivialities. With the rise of the virtuoso conductor, the demise of home music making, and the ease with which composers can make names for themselves, the practice of music "has been profaned." Further, the phenomenon of specialization has resulted in the separation of the skills that once resided in the single performer-composer. An overloaded, unnatural music that delights in technique for its own sake is the outcome. The public and critics alike, who are in no position to judge such supposedly meaningful music on a single hearing, are misled about its worth, whereas performers and conductors feel obliged to perform it. After having described the existing situation, Riemann proposes an antidote on the model of Johannes Brahms, a composer who, in his recognition of the worth and relevance of music as ancient as that of the Renaissance, parallels the young discipline of Musikwissenschaft, represented prominently by Riemann himself.

Hugo Riemann: Degeneration and Regeneration in Music

"How magnificently have we progressed in our day!" ["Wie herrlich weit haben wir es doch heute gebracht!"][1]

Really? In what respect?

Indeed we have progressed in the support of large concert orchestras in all our midsized cities — orchestras which 150 years ago numbered scarcely more than three in the world. And we have as well a great number of very respectable military and garden bands of all ability levels. With pride we can look back on a time when Vienna had no other permanent performance establishment than the Augarten concerts under Schuppanzigh,[2] made possible by the participation of amateurs, and when Berlin possessed not a single concert hall! In fact, concert life experienced such a phenomenal escalation in the course of the nineteenth century that the daily newspapers have had to double or triple the number of their music correspondents, just in order to be able to report on all the better musical performances. Aristocratic courts and the salons of wealthy patrons, which yet in the eighteenth century were nearly the only places where wandering artists could find recognition and remuneration, have fallen far back into second place. Devout music making in the home [das andächtige häusliche Musizieren] has all but ceased, and the mass training of the conservatories puts onto the concert stage even those who used to form the personnel of the private quartets and other small domestic ensembles, thus subjecting them to professional criticism. The entire practice of music has taken on a public character and thus has been profaned.[3] No one any longer wants to hide his light under a bushel. Even one who has achieved only modest results as a player, singer, or composer covets the laurel wreath, yet at a high price. Furthermore, a species of artist completely unknown in former times sits like the Olympian gods on the throne of this excess-ridden, modern concert life — the great conductors. Fantastic honoraria, such as were formerly paid only to the most world-renowned singers and certainly never bestowed upon composers, are thrust upon them, and such fees boost immeasurably the quality of their accomplishments in the eye of the public, which perceives value in terms of price. But these new gods are no longer content with local places of offering: they parade in triumph from city to city, from country to country, and demand tribute. The tours of the vocal and instrumental virtuosi are forced to take a backseat to those of the conductors (where possible complete with their entire orchestras). Single appearances of even quite respectable artists tend no longer, despite all their expensive publicity, to attract a good audience. One after another searches about for a modest living wage and bids farewell to a life of touring.

But the composers, too, complain more and more that, despite the enormous proliferation of concert ventures, their "novelities" nevertheless too seldom get a hearing. The union of composer and conductor in a single person, at one time proven so practical, has since the middle of the nineteenth century been discredited by "Kapellmeistermusik,"[4] and today one requires of a truly great conductor that, above all, he himself not indulge in composition. A great composer no longer becomes a Kapellmeister. Everything has its reason. One no longer trusts that composers, either by profession or by ambition, would have the magnanimity sufficient to bring deserved recognition to the works of other composers. The great figures of the baton are little persuaded to endanger the halo of their own fame by the failure of new music. Therefore the very greatest conductors, just as formerly the great virtuosi, remain with a tried and true repertory, whereas experiments with new music, although convention renders them not entirely avoidable, are better restricted.

The quality of the new music itself is relevant to the situation, as well. Seen by light of day, the new compositional achievements are missing the unimpeachable, overwhelming seriousness [Größe] that would be able to convince the conductors, in their natural role as art's servants. The most prominent characteristic of the new music with which the great conductors experiment is doubtless an excessively increased demand on the technical ability of orchestras and their leaders, an ability that the latter take great pains to display. It appears that neither composer nor conductor has considered that the poor audience — despite the best intentions and its exposure ahead of time to critical discussions, program notes, and so on — is not able to find its way through this mass of sound or to unravel its complications during a performance that passes by so swiftly; the listener cannot crack, quickly and one after another, the auditory nuts that rain down massively upon him. But after a few attempts of this sort, the conductor very wisely withdraws himself from the situation, if the press has not already succeeded in convincing the public that he is to be blamed for its not having grasped the magnitude and significance of the work. In the long run, though, these extorted successes certainly cannot last, even though it is possible to cite examples where such deception has persisted for years. A composer who today is able to write music in the grand style [Musik großen Stils] has every reason to expect to be buried with his manuscripts. Only in the less significant genres is it possible today to meet with success in this respect. It is now suddenly the sign of the times, if one wishes to be recognized by the upper 10,000 of the musical world, to avoid natural simplicity and to attract attention to oneself through all sorts of exaggerations; difficult notation; technical impediments to performance; expansion of the orchestral corpus; amassing of simultaneous, interlocking, and confused melodic lines, as well as of blurred harmonies; all where possible with express reference to the most modern and extravagent products of poetry or painting.

Given these conditions, if there is a critic of renown who, deceived by the "modern" behavior of the composer, regards the latter as the great man of the future and accordingly draws attention to him in a few enthusiastic articles, then sooner or later one or another conductor will feel obliged to venture the introduction of a work before the public. In 99 out of 100 cases, the result is the well-known disappointment of the public, which quickly cools the affectionate warmth of the conductor.

At the moment, then, conditions have fundamentally deteriorated. No one knows anymore the difference between the cook and the wine-cellar master. Since the deaths of Wagner and Liszt, there is on the side of the progressive party [auf Seite der vorwärtsdrängenden Partei] no authoritative personality who would be in a position to bridle the unchecked youth, no one who by decree and personal example would be able to demarcate the limits which ought not be transgressed. Therefore anarchy spreads, and "confusion in music" appears. Tragically, the conservative element, which still 20 years ago comprised a healthy balance to the hotspurs of progress, has forfeited all strength. Why have the achievements of Edvard Grieg,[5] Max Bruch,[6] Heinrich Hofmann,[7] Friedrich Kiel,[8] and Joseph Rheinberger[9] disappeared from the concert hall? The great works of Herzogenberg appeared too late to have been placed seriously in the running.[10] The unexpectedly swift demise of these great figures — as well as of Raff,[11] Rubinstein,[12] and Volkmann[13] — has robbed the surviving conservatives of all credibility, and the moderns charge, in the wake of the most extreme, as well as out ahead of it, into the abyss as in a mad witches' sabbath.

Degeneration and decadence are clear, and a complete detour, the debacle of modernity, stands directly in our path. Sober voices counsel a change in course, and courageous friends of the truth pull at the edge of the robes that enfold the wobbly bones of the rider to the left.

Is it too late?

It is never too late, at least not for those who do not join the insane ride into ruination. A lone gnarled oak trunk, with its powerful, deep roots, has held its footing in the path of the devastating hurricane. Its crown is undamaged and proudly stretches itself out ever more broadly. It tells the present where the salvation of the future lies; it reveals the healthy, nourishing soil of new strength. It is no coincidence that the only composer of the second half of the nineteenth century whose music has not vanished from the programs of the best concerts, but rather claims an ever stronger hold on them, is Johannes Brahms. Brahms began as an enthusiastic follower of the progressive efforts of the New Germans and gradually became a guardian of all traditions, nay, even an apologist for the appreciation of the worth of past artistic periods. As an artistic power he is the complement to the historicizing endeavors of the musicology that has developed in the last decades.

With secret concern that has gradually built into open hate, the radical progressives have seen these endeavors sprout and grow strong. Already now it is becoming evident that their instinct detected a dangerous enemy, because already the general public has begun to recognize that the rubble of past centuries has buried not only visual art of lofty beauty, but also that the music of the present in no way categorically surpasses or depreciates that of the past. Gluck, Handel, and Bach have been resurrected behind Beethoven, Mozart, and Haydn as the foremost masters of the immediate past, and behind them rise up Palestrina and Lasso as witnesses of a still much more remote time, the great music of which, though seeming foreign at first, must and will be exemplary to present and future generations, just as the art of the Renaissance is to the visual arts.

Brahms has already turned his artisanship to both periods, that of the eighteenth and sixteenth centuries, and he has given us an example of how our degenerate art can and must regenerate itself. The rich treasures of these long-since-faded epochs are inexhaustible, and therefore we would be thoroughly mistaken to search for the salvation of the immediate future's music in an imitation of Brahms — but following him along the path of a thorough study of the ancients is in fact the way that will lead us out of the chaos of the present aesthetic. Not only for their own value must the works of the past be recovered and made accessible to the present, but also for the return to health of our decadent and degenerate production, and for the regeneration of our whole sense of musical feeling. Therefore this creativity from the youthful spring of the true, earnest art of all times is indispensable not only for composers, but also for the reeducation of performers and audiences.

6

Degeneration and Regeneration in Music

Neue Musik-Zeitung 29/3 (31 October 1907): 49–51

Introduction

"I've just completed an essay that will hit like a small bomb; it will appear on 15 October in the 'Neue Musikzeitung'! In it I have *violently settled accounts* with the regressives!" (letter of 29 September 1907 in Popp and Shigihara 1995: 203).[1] Reger's words to Henri Hinrichsen announce his intent to take up cudgels against Riemann, in the form of a protracted essay in which he aims to answer his former mentor point by point, and which amounts to the low watermark in what had been a difficult relationship since the mid 1890s. Both the length and the tone of the article suggest the strong feelings bound up in Reger's relationship with Riemann, and it hardly can be read as an objective response to the latter, who had in any case not mentioned the composer or his music. On 1 April 1907, Reger had taken up duties as University Music Director at the University of Leipzig, where Riemann had been active since 1895. The present essay, then, may be read as a kind of declaration of independence at the very time Reger joined the Leipzig faculty, and on the eve of his being granted a professorship by the Saxon king Friedrich August III. Not surprisingly, the essay evinces a conflicted attitude toward academia and scholarship, for which Riemann and his theories serve, in Reger's mind, as the locus classicus. "My goals *differ so fundamentally* from Riemann's that we will never find common ground *artistically*," Reger would write to Fritz Stein in 1909 (letter of 16 July 1909 in Popp 1982: 59).

Whereas it is clear that pupil and mentor still agreed on certain points — the lamentable state of domestic music making, for instance, or the negative effects attendant upon the emergence of the specialized, virtuoso conductor — much of what Riemann had advanced touched raw nerves with Reger. Riemann's talk of "extorted successes" for new orchestral works, the complications of which "rain down" in a "mass of sound" upon audiences, may well have recalled for Reger the problematical reception of his *Sinfonietta* op. 90 in the autumn of 1905. Certainly, Reger took Riemann's description of scores that "avoid natural simplicity" as a direct condemnation of his own music. Further, he reacts strongly against Riemann's suggestion that Brahms's art and the aims of academia are cut from the same tree: in reply, Reger wants to say that notions of tradition and progress in art do not turn on blind quasi-artistic credos to Brahms or Wagner, or to absolute or program music, respectively. Hence, Reger can act as a sympathetic emissary for the camp of Strauss without himself having to pursue the composition of Lisztian symphonic poems, a rhetorical move that appears to have taken Riemann off guard.

Degeneration and Regeneration in Music

With this title, Professor Dr. *Hugo Riemann* has just published an extended essay in *Max Hesse's Deutscher Musikerkalender* for 1908. The views and "advice" developed therein compel me to illuminate them from the standpoint of the *forward-striving* musician. One might possibly still grant certain points made by Professor Dr. H. Riemann regarding the fashion for conductor-virtuosi, a fashion that bears fruit in our own day. But our vocal and instrumental virtuosi are surely not, as Herr Professor Dr. Riemann believes, so "poor" that they — one after the other — must search about for a "modest" (?!) living wage. Precisely today's increasingly richer musical culture [unser sich immer reicher gestaltendes Musikleben] demands many more soloists of all types than in former times, so that Herr Professor Dr. Riemann's viewpoint here contradicts reality.

Herr Professor Dr. Riemann then writes further that composers, too, complain that their "novelties" get a hearing all too seldom, despite the huge increase of concert ventures. This assertion of Professor Dr. Riemann likewise *in no way* corresponds to the facts. In particular composers alive today have little reason — in comparison to "the good old days" — to complain about a lack of such opportunities. It has not been that long ago that even the most significant composers were "old men" before they were "concert worthy"! Brahms and Wagner were truly long enough banned from our concert halls. The programs of our time, though, undeniably demonstrate that the performance societies (with fewer and fewer exceptions) have come to understand that one *must* make allowance for living composers, too — and even in the most reactionary cities, where 20–30 years ago one cried out bitterly if a work of Wagner or Brahms "strayed" into a program, one today programs Strauss, Mahler, and — ††† Reger.

Of course the critics, the patrimonious resident "musicology," still often scold out of indignation, but they nevertheless cannot hinder the fact that even in these cities with "critical oil lamp lighting," a good many followers assemble around the freshly waving banner of the "new composers" — admittedly not from the circles of the moss-covered heads. Alone the Genossenschaft deutscher Tonsetzer (Anstalt für musikalisches Aufführungsrecht),[2] of undeniably meritorious service to us living composers, is the most convincing proof that Riemann's orientation in this matter is *completely false.*

Herr Professor Dr. H. Riemann writes further: "The most prominent characteristic of the new music with which the great conductors experiment is doubtless an excessively increased demand on the technical ability of orchestras and their leaders, an ability that the latter take great pains to display.... It is now suddenly the sign of the times, if one wishes to be recognized by the upper 10,000 of the musical world, to avoid natural simplicity and to attract attention to oneself through all sorts of exaggerations; difficult notation; technical impediments to performance; expansion of the orchestral corpus; amassing of simultaneous, interlocking, and confused melodic lines, as well as of blurred harmonies; all where possible with express reference to the most modern and extravagent products of poetry or painting."

We must clarify particularly regarding the sentence "... to avoid natural simplicity and...through all sorts of exaggerations; difficult notation," etc. *In this Herr Professor Riemann is entirely correct.* For 15 years there have existed editions of the masterworks of Bach, Mozart, Beethoven, etc., etc. which in fact were prepared exclusively according to the principle "... to avoid natural simplicity and...through all sorts of exaggerations; difficult notation," etc.! *Curiously enough, these editions are —— by Hugo Riemann* (see Figure 6.1).[3]

Concerning the amassing of technical difficulties that we ††† moderns espouse only in order to awaken the interest of the superficially minded public — by the way, certainly a strange opinion of the "integrity" of our artistic convictions — I will allow myself as a non–music historian to remark modestly that Bach's music, for example, because of its amassing of technical difficulties, was considered so unplayable that one believed that Bach alone could perform his works. Furthermore, did not old Papa Haydn, perhaps about 110 years ago, earnestly advise the young Beethoven against publishing the three piano sonatas op. 2 because — they were supposedly too difficult to play. So here too the "technical impediments to performance"! — Poor Beethoven! — Were not precisely Beethoven's very greatest works — the last sonatas and string quartets — considered unplayable for nearly a generation? And Brahms! I still can remember from my youth how one swore and grumbled about the difficult accompaniments in the Brahms Lieder. So, here too: technical impediments to performance! Poor Brahms, you really should read "Degeneration and Regeneration in Music" (*Deutscher Musikerkalender* 1908), so that you might finally become aware of your base sins against the Holy Spirit of German musicology!

Figure 6.1 Johann Sebastian Bach: Invention in F minor BWV 780, in Hugo Riemann, ed., *Joh. Seb. Bach's. Inventionen mit genauer Bezeichnung der Phrasierung und neuem Fingersatz* (Leipzig: Kahnt, 1887) with Reger's (?) analysis in the sense of Riemann.

Then Herr Professor Dr. H. Riemann advances against us moderns the old story, an argument that remains just as new as it continues to prove itself false. (By the way, our modern polyphony, for example, is utterly modest when one thinks of the intricate [ungeheuer] polyphony the old Netherlandish masters employed in their works.) At long last, it is really necessary to assert clearly and emphatically that all the reproaches which Herr Professor Dr. Riemann levels against us very "lively" ["lebendige"] underminers of the past — for which he in any case offers no substantiation — have *again* and *again* been flung with fiery latitude and classical crudity, etc., etc. precisely at *those figures* who, after a few decades, were praised before the reasonable as saviors from delivery into the bleakest epigonism. Has one, and have the Herren musicologists, really forgotten, that Bach appeared so "incomprehensible" to his time, that he was actually recognized during his own lifetime *not* as a composer, but rather *only* as a virtuoso? How much abuse did the divinely favored Mozart have to endure? Was it not said that he — Mozart — composed too "densely" and orchestrated too "noisily"?!

And how did the German critics behave toward Beethoven? Did not the majority of Beethoven's contemporaries consider him completely insane? I cite here an assessment of the great Leonore overture: *"rhapsodies of an incurable madman!"* [*"Rhapsodien eines unheilbar dem Wahnsinn Verfallenen!"*] (And one could introduce here hundreds of similar views from "professional circles.") How many difficult battles had to transpire before, for instance, Schumann achieved his "breakthrough"?! (He himself of course did not live to see this.) Have the immensely dire years of suffering of a R. Wagner been forgotten already? Have even the Herren music historians forgotten them?

And Brahms: were not all Brahms's symphonies received at their first hearing with icy remoteness? And Bruckner and Hugo Wolf? Was it not E. Hanslick who regarding Bruckner could write with cold blood the beautiful words: "This music stinks!"[4] (By the way, Hanslick also wrote many books on music!) And when one compares the critiques that have been written in abundance *against* Beethoven, *against* Schubert, Schumann, Wagner, Brahms, Bruckner, and H. Wolf — when one compares these to that with which Herr Professor Dr. Riemann's protest seeks to brand the devilish moderns, one finds a remarkable similarity: *it is the battle waged by those who no longer have anything to contribute against the impetuous progressives!* — But hail, hail to those who are "evaluated" in the same way that the great immortal figures were once evaluated! It is an extraordinary honor for us disciples who, our health unaffected by the tuberculor pallor of remote theory, plant our trees in the eternally blossoming forest of German art with fresh daring and faith in the Germanic spirit.

Herr Professor Dr. Riemann writes further: "Since the deaths of Wagner and Liszt, there is on the side of the progressive party no authoritative personality who would be in a position to bridle the unchecked youth, no one who by decree and personal example would be able to demarcate the limits which ought not be transgressed!"

No, Herr Professor, that makes us laugh! It would be a very sad sign of *actual degeneration* if our youth, in an urge toward activity, to venture the unimagined and the unheard, denied themselves and instead made rigorously pious, innocent kindergarten music! (As an aside, it is really quite amusing that Herr Professor Riemann has suddenly declared Fr. Liszt, to whom he denied any actual creative talent,[5] an authority for the impetuous younger generation and regrets deeply that Liszt no longer bridles the unchecked youth.) Certainly, if the time were to come when the youth would lose their futuristically oriented ideals, so that they would not aim beyond the target — certainly, *then would* stand before us, as I have said, *an irreparable degeneration in the very worst sense*. By the way: who then bridled Bach, Beethoven, Schumann, Wagner, Brahms? Did not the great ones appear to their time terribly "unbridled"?

Further: "...to demarcate the limits which ought not be transgressed!" What does this mean? Have not absolutely *all* of our great and immortal figures ruthlessly and with mighty fists advanced into the eternal the limits as understood in their time, that the contemporary aesthetic fixed "paralyzed" ["kreuzlahm"] in place? (Admittedly very much to the irreparable vexation of the guilded intellectuals [der zünftigen Schriftgelehrten]! And we living ones, who are *no* Beethoven, Schubert, Schumann, Wagner, Brahms, H. Wolf — *we nevertheless do not allow ourselves to be bridled, we will not be muzzled and placed under musicological guardianship!* — — —

Then Herr Professor Dr. Riemann grumbles nostalgically about the past accomplishments of E. Grieg, M. Bruch, H. Hofmann, Friedrich Kiel, and Joseph Rheinberger! Does he not know that the successes of these composers have so quickly faded only because they did not achieve *enough individuality*, because they obviously were *too* dependent on the older generations? Only the individual, the mental capacity [der seelische Gehalt] that emanates from an individual, is the guarantee of immortality.

According to Herr Professor Dr. Riemann's view, we moderns stand at the brink of debacle. Presently we will, as he writes, plunge into the abyss, and when one pulls at the edge of the robes that enfold "the wobbly bones of the rider to the left,"[6] then — does there likely grin a hollow skull of death!? Oh, how grim and gruesome! It reminds one immediately of a wax museum, where one can see the most dreadful things for 50 cents' admission. Herr Professor Dr. Riemann: *We riders to the left with wobbly bones absolutely do not fear the plunge into the abyss! We sit firmly in the saddle, we riders to the left! You* will *much sooner* plunge into the abyss with your attacks, the proof of which you yourself have provided!

In all seriousness: Does Hugo Riemann really believe that we — Strauss, Mahler, Pfitzner, etc. and finally my humble self — venture out on our ride into the "uncertain" in such "directionless" fashion that we allow ourselves to be carried by our muse, completely unprepared, into a realm not accessible to everyone, that we stray without principle from one phantom to another? Does Herr Professor Dr. Riemann not know that we — in the same way as he — harbor artistic conviction matured particularly through practical experience, not through dusty book wisdom? If Riemann *knew* [*kennen*] what we have written here, then he *would have* to know that our musical-technical knowledge stands at least equal to that of a Max Bruch or Joseph Rheinberger! Does he really live under the erroneous impression that we have sacrilegiously cast all the old masters overboard? Or has it not yet become clear *to him* that every period must naturally have its *corresponding artistic* expression? Has Wagner in all his works, *Richard Strauss* in *Don Juan*, *Till Eulenspiegel*, *Tod und Verklärung* — have not these already become altogether classical? (Please stone me!) Has not an almost incalculable number of precisely the *best* modern musicians rallied under our soiled and spotted banner with the most sincere enthusiasm? Are *all* these people so blinded that they have lost the daylight of true art???

Herr Professor Dr. Riemann writes further: "A lone gnarled oak trunk, with its powerful, deep roots, has held its footing in the path of the devastating hurricane (namely J. Brahms)... As an artistic power he is the complement to the historicizing endeavors of the musicology that has developed in the last decades!"

I believe that my complete admiration of Joh. Brahms and my glowing veneration for the great old masters is too well known that I would need to emphasize this again in the present context. But above all I *protest* here *most energetically* against the notion of Brahms as the complement to the historicizing endeavors of the musicology that has developed in the last decades! It is a great, great error if Herr Professor Dr. Riemann believes that on this account Brahms has become the gnarled oak trunk that has endured the hurricanes. Brahms as the complement to the musicology of his time!! No, that is divinely discerning! It is well known that musicology only seizes on a great figure once the cool grass has at long last overgrown him. Once about 100 or 200 years have past, only then is such an old master palatable. Or does the affair lie differently in the Collegium musicum?[7] It would be very sad for the immortality of a Brahms if he owed his status in the first place to his reliance on the old masters, as Riemann believes. Such an assertion could only issue from remote theory, which runs its lonely circles aside from the golden stream of life, from the vigorously pulsating heart's blood of our time! And the most conclusive proof *against* Professor Dr. Riemann's view is a figure, for instance, like Rheinberger! Whoever is familiar with his development, whoever is aware of his comings and goings in Munich, knows that Rheinberger had *at least* the same strong sympathy with the old masters as that of J. Brahms! But *despite all this*, Rheinberger has withered so quickly![8] What assures Brahms's immortality is *never and in no case* the "reliance" on old masters, rather *only* the fact that he knew how to set free new, unexpected emotions *of the soul* [daß er neue ungeahnte *seelische* Stimmungen auszulösen wußte], on the basis of his own soul-centered personality [seiner eigenen seelischen Persönlichkeit]! *Therein* lies the root of all immortality, but *never* in the mere reliance on the old masters, which the inexorable dynamic of history will form into a death sentence in a few decades!

Herr Dr. Riemann writes further: "With secret concern that has gradually built into open hate, the radical progressives have seen these endeavors (namely those "historicizing" endeavors of musicology) sprout and grow strong," etc.

Again, the situation is not that severe. If the efforts of musicology are based *solely* on the motivation of bringing honor to the old masters, then we radical progressives have every reason *to greet* these efforts *with extreme sympathy*! I believe myself able to assume that among the radical progressives, not a one has acted out of hate toward these meritorious efforts. If this nevertheless has occurred, then the offending party has already stricken himself from the list of those who are to be taken seriously. One may, however, assume with "considerable" certainty that we progressives are much more frequently greeted with hate, both open and concealed. It may certainly have transpired that the "wobbly bones of the riders to the left" have trodden, in sarcastic black humor and sometimes not unjustly, on those who themselves have never sat in the saddle or have only a very imperfect command of riding, if one has tugged all too fondly at the "edge of the robes" of the maddest riders.

Finally, Herr Professor Dr. Riemann writes that our degenerate art can and must regenerate itself. What then do we horrible moderns want other than regeneration — of course on *our* terms! Standing still is impossible, and a real degeneration in the most genuine sense of the word would arise if, over and over again, such "characters" did not step up to regenerate, stubbornly and daringly, in their way! Fresh blood, new life, and new goals have never done damage; undeniably, in all periods they have proven themselves the sole measure against *actual* decadence!

Naturally, Herr Professor Dr. Riemann is convinced that we find ourselves today in an utterly dreadful "confusion in music"! For several months, this "confusion" has caused a great stir. People have written about it, they have hypocriticized to blue heaven, without altering anything about the "confusion"! In my opinion, the "confusion," so suddenly discovered, commenced with *Salome.* The entire musical world — of course with the exception of a few "hillbillies" ["Hinterwäldler"] — had grown accustomed to the works of Richard Strauss. Gradually, the conviction had made headway that Strauss is undoubtedly the most significant representative of the "symphonic poem" since Franz Liszt. Suddenly appeared *Salome*, and with it the "confusion"! How curious! Is then the Strauss of *Salome* another person, a completely transformed creative mind? In no case! One must not have understood Strauss so correctly, if one "shrieks" only now, after his important works like *Don Juan*, *Till Eulenspiegel*, *Tod und Verklärung*, even [*Ein*] *Heldenleben* for years have been a steadfast part and parcel, so to speak, of our programs, after they have become absolute "classics" in their own right.

After the stake has been erected on which, to the inner delight of all conservatives, I am to be roasted, I would like to ease my conscience from something that has long weighed it down: Among the riders are those who with "reflection" look down on Schumann and Mendelssohn. It seems to me that these people will be recognized by a later generation at most as underaged "Mendel's children" ["Mendelskinder"] or "decrepit Mendel's women" ["altersschwache Mendelsweiber"]. Their course bends too gently, far too gently, to the left, since we "genuine" riders to the left know all too well how Schumann and even Mendelssohn — each in his own way — rode hard to the left, and we "genuine" riders to the left renounce *none* of our own! — (Now the fire for me will probably be lit from the left as well!)

I deeply regret that I *must* place myself with my artistic convictions so much in opposition to the views of my former mentor, to whom I render the most thorough admiration as by far the most excellent theorist not only of our time, but also since Rameau! But there is a great, if razor-sharp, difference between theory and the powerfully forward rushing quality in our music since Liszt and Wagner! And despite my generally known "unqualified," immeasurable veneration and admiration for all of our old, great masters without exception, I can say according to my conviction and judgment — although I do not know whether my outward stature suggests "wobbly bones" — *"I ride unyieldingly to the left!"*[9]

Leipzig, October 1907
Max Reger[10]

Part III
Reception

7

Hugo Wolf's Artistic Legacy

Süddeutsche Monatshefte 1/2 (1904): 157–64

Introduction

"Hugo Wolfs künstlerischer Nachlass" appeared in February 1904 in the second issue of the new *Süddeutsche Monatshefte*, at the request of the periodical's editor Paul Nikolaus Cossmann. Reger had taken a serious interest in Wolf by 1898 at the latest, having published four of the *Mörike-Lieder* in arrangements for voice and organ with the Mannheim Verlag of Heckel. By 1900, the younger composer would dedicate the *Zwölf Lieder* op. 51 (on texts of Morgenstern, Bierbaum, and Dehmel, among others) to Wolf. In 1908, Reger arranged ten further Lieder by Wolf, this time from the *Spanisches Liederbuch*, for voice and organ, these appearing with the four previous *Mörike-Lieder* of 1898 issued by C. F. Peters. At the time of the following article, Reger was intensively occupied with editing and arranging several works from Wolf's estate acquired by Lauterbach and Kuhn, and the essay may be read as a companion to that activity.

Here, Reger seizes on the opportunity provided by the first anniversary of Wolf's death (22 February) to reflect on the composer's position in contemporary German musical life. Such reflection, however, facilitates a larger agenda. By casting Wolf as an artist marginalized and underappreciated during his lifetime who finds a more positive, if superficial, reception only after his death, Reger draws attention to the incompetence of the critics, the capricious way in which the views of the public are formed, and the lot of the suffering, "serious" composer.

The Wolf essay is apparently the only one for which a manuscript survives. The autograph of twenty-one pages (see Figure 7.1) is held by the Max Reger Institute (Karlsruhe) and has been reproduced in facsimile under the editorship of Ottmar Schreiber (Schreiber 1966). Although the autograph text reflects the published article in most points, the two differ throughout in both insignificant and substantial details, and it is not possible to ascertain precisely the former's role in the production of the latter. When the article has appeared in later sources, it has always reproduced the text of the published essay (ibid.; Hasse 1921: 179–90; Wilske 1995: 339–44), and even Schreiber gives this version opposite the reproduced original. Although the present translation rests on the printed version, I have indicated substantive differences with Reger's manuscript.

Hugo Wolf's Artistic Legacy

It would be a very interesting experiment to establish how often Hugo Wolf's name is represented in the programs of our Lieder recitals and other concerts between the years 1893 and 1903. The results of this investigation, which admittedly would not be so easy to carry out, would be absolutely dumbfounding, even for those musicians who have supported innovative programming over the last ten years. Completely unknown a decade ago, and today recognized, admired, and celebrated as Franz Schubert's friend and kindred spirit! Even the public everywhere is beginning to — buy — Hugo Wolf's songs. Our

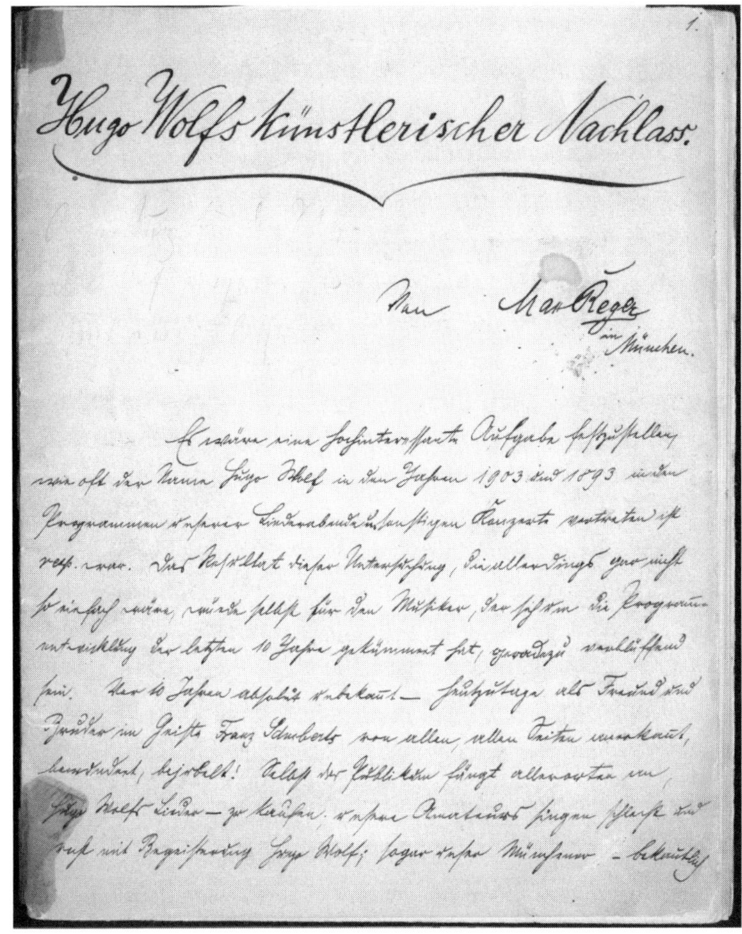

1.

Hugo Wolfs künstlerischer Nachlass.

Von Max Reger in München.

Figure 7.1 Max Reger: "Hugo Wolf's Artistic Legacy," autograph page 1.

amateurs enthusiastically sing Hugo Wolf as well as they are able. Even our Munich court theater, which is well known for staging — pardon, postponing — dozens of new things, performed *Corregidor*[1] most successfully, and a number of other court and city theaters likewise intend to offer this opera to their "Wolf-hungry" public during the present season. Our daily papers and scholarly journals publish countless discussions of, and essays about, Hugo Wolf. Shortly, the first monument to this celebrated composer is to be unveiled in Vienna,[2] and — oh sublime achievement! — there are even picture postcards for sale with Hugo Wolf's portrait! Hugo Wolf's art finds itself truly in the most splendid, unique, insurpassable state.

But what was Hugo Wolf's condition in 1893?

Our German history of art, which as it already has at its disposal an imposing number of the most blameless and nevertheless very tragic disgraces — I recall the cases of Bach, Mozart, Beethoven, Schubert, Schumann, Wagner, and Bruckner — can with justifiable pride count the case of Hugo Wolf among its treasures. Such a treasure can never be eaten by moths [nie von Motten zerfressen werden können]: these disgraces are immortal.[3] It has not been long since a critical essay from Berlin gave Hugo Wolf the honorable title of a "diminished 6/4 chord fad-monger" [eines "verminderten Quartsextaccordfexen"] and said of the most accessible, charming works of the composer that "repeated hearings would not help these songs."[4] For some time it was considered folly to sing Hugo Wolf, and with very few exceptions, our singers could not be convinced to include even one song of the diminished 6/4 chord fad-monger in their repertory. Even serious musicians cast pitiful smiles at those who did not speak the name of Hugo Wolf with a satirical tone. It has been said of an influential musician, recently mourned in all the newspapers, that he gave the classic answer to a request to perform Hugo Wolf: "No, I will not make a fool of myself."[5]

Our good German public of course believed and continues to believe everything that is put before it by undiscerning critics (the very honorable exceptions to which I wish expressly to recognize here, by the way) in countless scathing discussions about the composer. And given a similar case, this same public would behave today, a year after Hugo Wolf's death, in exactly the same way again. (Witness Hans Pfitzner!)[6] Even the Berlin music critic who recently called Beethoven's great B-flat major Sonata (Hammerklavier) [no. 29, op. 106] an "étude not suited to concert performance" was not able to shake the German newspaper reader's beliefs, which alone confer salvation.[7] It is really much, much easier to read the judgment of Herr X in the long-standing prominent newspaper, to accept it, to allow oneself to be "led about like sheep"; it is much more difficult to form one's own opinion on the basis of exacting knowledge and true understanding. With what malicious satisfaction did one read there that this Hugo Wolf takes leave of convention in composing songs that are completely different from those justifiably so beloved, singable, and pleasing songs of Hildach, Meyer-Hellmund, etc.[8] And in that case one completely overlooked the fact that it would have been much more honorable for the critics if they had brought their own critical impotence to light in a civilized manner,[9] rather than having run about like roosters with a scolding tone as they did in the case of Hugo Wolf.

Let us not be surprised! There are still people today who leave the concert hall with bittersweet facial expressions when a work of Brahms is played. And others, some of whom want to be musicians or even composers, sit during a Brahms work in such disquiet that one would think they had drunk tainted sour wine. Recall the enthusiasm with which our public recently greeted "Überbrettl";[10] still today it is enchanted by many "Überbrettl" songs, compositions of unbelievable banality and vulgarity.[11] With what greed are all those "wicked," horrible songs devoured which certain composers throw upon the market, with enviable pecuniary success.

But how does Hugo Wolf, this secluded, deeply introspective tone poet, reconcile himself with the undeniable fact of deteriorating taste? And yet, one cannot deny that Hugo Wolf, who curried neither the favor of the people nor the recognition of his contemporaries, has become stylish! A few weeks ago the papers announced that a large publishing firm has acquired the rights to a portion of Hugo Wolf's songs at the price of 200,000 marks.[12] The composer never in his life took in as much for the whole of his work as the yearly interest on this purchase price.[13] These days it is fashionable to rave about Hugo Wolf. Whether this is accompanied by understanding or knowledge does not matter; no one asks about that. The point is that the raving takes place and that thereby one bestows upon oneself a distinguished air. A great number of years and much effort is required, however, before Hugo Wolf becomes to the German people what Schubert and Schumann are. May those of our presses that have for years held the composer's banner high never be discouraged: may they again and again call attention to the tone poet Hugo Wolf in enlightening ways, so that we might see the day when he is no longer stylish, but rather ruler in the song-steeped hearts of the German people.

The treasures which this God-gifted musician has left us are evident, and they need only be pointed out with enthusiasm and the happiest admiration. In this respect, though, one ought not forget that we possess not only valuable songs from him, but that he has given us most precious creations in almost every musical genre. These nearly completely unknown works, which have become accessible to the public only since the death of their author, will certainly be granted a better lot than that of his vocal works in the beginning. Their creator has, after all, passed away, and thereby the chief condition for one's performing, applauding, and celebrating these works is fulfilled.

In his choral work *Christnacht* (von Platen)[14] for mixed chorus and orchestra, Hugo Wolf offers our choral societies a task that cannot be warmly enough commended to them. The treatment of the choir is, as to be expected, masterly; nowhere does the composer place remarkable demands on the abilities of the singers. Despite the almost constant homophonic treatment of the chorus, it maintains an attractive character, most successfully supported by sensitive orchestration. Proficient church choirs and secular choruses should, in order to raise the level of their sometimes quite dreary repertory, sing diligently the six *Geistliche Lieder nach Gedichten von Josef von Eichendorff* (a capella; like the other works addressed here, appearing with Lauterbach and Kuhn in Leipzig). These are really excellent choral things, from which it is difficult to single out the most beautiful, since they all bear witness to a most potent originality. These same choruses appear also in an arrangement for men's choir,[15] and it would be truly refreshing if by way of these earnest songs — completely averse to everything shallow and superficial — a proper breach could be made in the Chinese wall of incompetent song production. If thereby the *Deutsches Lied* of the Bohemian composer Wenzeslaus Kalliwoda[16] were to disappear entirely, this would not be a particular misfortune. Hothouse patriotism will not prosper! Unfortunately there has appeared to date only one choral society that has become somewhat acquainted with these magnificent works.[17]

Furthermore, it would be very welcome if our string quartets would play the String Quartet in D minor,[18] a work from the composer's youth left behind by him and discovered, as it were, by accident. This piece, which unmistakeably bears all the traits of a youthful work, nevertheless contains so many beautiful and interesting things that it ought to appear quite often on programs, if only for pedagogical reasons. From here, one could easily build a bridge to the later, true Hugo Wolf. I have already implied that the work[19] has deficiencies. In the first place, an undeniable and very striking ignorance of string quartet composition is occasionally encountered. Likewise, the melodic construction is still somewhat unnatural in certain passages. One senses what the composer wanted and could not achieve because of a lack of purely technical ability [das rein technische Können]. Here and there the purity of the texture falls short. However, an austere, deeply felt passion of the tonal language compensates for this, a sweeping temperament which impetuously strikes out a course in the first and last movements, particularly. And everywhere one already finds the true Wolf in passages that only he could have conceived. I can befriend the recently published youthful songs with less ease. Of course it is of greatest interest to become acquainted with the very beginnings of Wolf's lyricism. But between these songs — appearing under the title *Aus der Jugendzeit*[20] — and those that Wolf himself published exists too great a difference to make advisable a transplanting of these youthful things into the concert environment. Only if one compares these beginnings of Wolf's lyricism with his mature song masterpieces does one divine with what inexorable self-criticism, what iron industry he must have worked, so that he obviously in fact had no time to bother with "inner experiences of the soul" [mit "seelischen und innerlichen Erlebnissen"]. One can guess, too, that he cannot be numbered among those pious composers who always worship only themselves. With respect to this enormous self-criticism, Hugo Wolf is a shining example to our youngest generation of composers, an example that cannot be meaningfully contemplated too often. Wolf's early Lieder teach the youngest titans (who give birth to symphonic poems, symphonies, and large-scale songs with only the largest orchestras at an age when other mortals are still adorning school benches) the fatal lesson: "Begin small, end big!"[21]

Hugo Wolf could bring about great things as a teacher as well.

Nevertheless, the publication of these early songs is to be regarded very favorably insofar as their ease of execution, the comfortably singable vocal part, and the nearly-always-simple piano accompaniment to some extent guarantees that the mass of the musical and unmusical public, which always looks for technically easier things, will find a place for them.

Among those unpublished works left behind by the composer, the *Italienische Serenade* for small orchestra, of which only the first movement exists in finished form, appears with the same publisher. This attractive work is among the most delightful examples of the entire serenade genre, and it will surely become a part of the regular repertory of all the better orchestras. This single movement — how unfortunate that we have only this one movement! — has such bewitching aural appeal and makes such charming, highly original use of orchestral color that it will certainly kindle greatest enthusiasm when subjected to subtle performance. I should draw the attention of orchestral conductors to the fact that, in order to enhance the effect of the piece, it is advisable to replace the solo viola with an alto oboe. Hugo Wolf himself has left us an arrangement of the work for string quartet.[22]

Hugo Wolf's symphonic poem *Penthesilea*[23] is undoubtedly the crowning work of all his orchestral compositions. Assuming that he had remained healthy, what could the master (who met such an early death) have further achieved in this so controversial field of the symphonic poem, attended to by so many talented and untalented composers alike? I regard his symphonic poem *Penthesilea* (after Heinrich Kleist's tragedy of the same name) as unquestionably one of the most significant, healthiest creations of the last decades. The themes are genial in their substance, and the invention never lags. Hugo Wolf never panders — in my opinion an advantage that cannot be too highly valued — to the stupor for mood music so beloved today, a kind of music that almost always aims at mere effect. Forgoing the superfluous, miserable, hackneyed manufacturing of artificial phrases, the wonderful poetry of the piece rushes by, bar for bar. Already the first theme, symbolizing the departure of the Amazons for Troy, is of an elemental force, convincingly intensified further in a gripping development. One should note how in this first section nearly all the themes of the whole work appear eventually, dialoguing contrapuntally in the most ingenious ways. The transition to a sharply contrasting, effective episode ("Der Traum Penthesileas vom Rosenfest") is highly original. Long, nobly shaped melodic lines, extremely light instrumentation, and very refined harmony (I hope not too perverse for certain ears) lend this episode a most penetrating poetic charm. A brief, increasingly passionate intensification leads to the section "Kämpfe, Leidenschaften,

Wahnsinn, Vernichtung," the zenith of the whole work. Hugo Wolf here brings to bear a characterful, keenly felt power of expression and a complete mastery of the technical aspect of composition, an accomplishment deserving of high praise. The steely harmonies gush down mercilessly; the motives are played off each other with eminent contrapuntal artistry. The raging tumult gradually calms in order to lead to a visionary emergence of the theme symbolizing the dream at the rose festival (score page 83). But Penthesilea's blessed dream does not last long; the language becomes more and more passionate, more and more pressing, only to culminate in a true ecstasy of rage. Hugo Wolf has realized here (particularly on page 89 of the score) an indescribable ability to characterize the diabolical. How the motives burst onto one another with an unheard-of boldness; how the harmony defies all the good old rules, stirring up so much wig powder; how everything intensifies so irresistably until the unshakeable, booming trombone motive of destruction crushes the wild ecstasy with elemental force. All this reminds us of what an irreparable loss the world of art has suffered in Hugo Wolf's death. After this monstrous musical catastrophe (score pages 105–110), the motive of Penthesilea's dream of the rose festival appears again in the strings, following upon the ghostly dissolution of the basses. The woodwinds take it up in the most delicate colors. There follows a renewed outbreak of the wildest despair, trampled by the merciless motive of destruction. Then appears in the divided first violins the musical symbol of the rose festival dream; muffled, sly gestures from the strings, and the mighty tragedy fades away with a long F-minor chord in the woodwinds and brass.

Had Hugo Wolf written only this one work, music history would have had to count him among the greatest of composers. It is therefore an outright joyful fact that this colossal work is to be given a number of performances already this winter (I know of 25).[24] Since the composer of *Penthesilea* is dead, his state of affairs is very favorable. Dead composers can no longer pose a threat, even to conductors who compose.

I heard a short while ago that a number of other works from Hugo Wolf's estate are supposed to have turned up. I know neither the genre of these works nor whether they are youthful or mature compositions. I have tried in vain to find out more about them. But as soon as I am in the happy position of having gotten my hands on these pieces, among them the opera fragment *Manuel Venegas*,[25] I will not hesitate to say a few words about them.

Perhaps Hugo Wolf's example will have the effect of unifying those who,[26] free from all partisan hatred, cliques, and backward tendencies, believe in the healthy, productive further development of our German music. If there still be musicians, composers, or narrower circles of composers who have, so to speak, put up a wall around themselves by societal or other associations, and for whom the figure of Hugo Wolf would be — like our efforts to popularize Wolf's art in the noblest, widest sense — uncomfortable or horrific, then we would like to give these people the assurance that we will not call up the gods in a vain fight against them. Considering his hard fate, it is deeply regrettable that Hugo Wolf did not leave behind a memoir, to which the following poem of Gustav Falke might have served as an introduction:

I will beat you with whips,
With flaming whips,
Until you cry out:
Stop,
We have committed a sacrilege!

[Mit Peitschen will ich euch schlagen
Mit flammenden Peitschen,
Bis ihr aufschreit:
Halt ein,
Wir haben gefrevelt!]

Where are the murdered souls,
The victims of your serpent-poisonous wisdom?
Carefree and happy, he jumped onto the scene,
The genius with the child's laugh,
His hands clapped pleasure
And his mouth voiced
songs of joy.

[Wo sind die gemordeten Seelen,
Die Opfer eurer schlangengiftigen Klugheit?
Leicht, froh sprang er ins Feld,
Der Genius mit dem Kinderlachen,

Seine Hand klatschte Lust
Und sein Mund tönte
Freudensgesänge.]
. . . .
And you struck him,
And crucified him with hunger
And laughed:
Behold, what a fool!

[Und ihr schlugt ihn,
Und kreuzigtet ihn mit Hunger
Und lachtet:
Seht, welch ein Narr!][27]

Because of the folly of earlier generations, the tragedy of genius will not repeat itself again.[28] The extent to which the musicians, not the larger public, are to blame for certain circumstances will not be addressed here. Perhaps one might recommend to those who are complacent or smug that they read the professional journals a bit more frequently; and one might suggest to editors that they listen somewhat more closely to artists with ability, not to the cries of markets and those who supply them. If public approval is the point, then of course the words of Hölderlin will always apply: "Ah, only what is good for the marketplace can please people.… To believe in the divine one must be divine in one's own right" ["Ach, der Menge gefällt, was auf den Marktplatz taugt. An das Göttliche glauben die allein, die es selber sind."][29]

8

On April 1

Neue Zeitschrift für Musik 71/14 (30 March 1904): 274–75

Introduction

"My Duncan article will become immediately intelligible to you," wrote Reger to the Berlin organist Walter Fischer,

> when you know that the *Münchner Neuste Nachrichten* has written that one can rightly understand Chopin only after one has seen Chopin danced by Duncan! Therefore my so repulsively bombastic tone in the idolization of Urschl's big toe — this tone is an *exact* copy of the tone in which almost *all* the local papers write about Duncan! (Letter of 12 April 1904 in Schreiber 1956: 141)

The American dancer Isadora Duncan (1877–1927) had come to Germany already in 1903 and began to present her free, improvisatory dance style there to the accompaniment of the musical "masterworks." Duncan herself did not have a particularly favorable initial impression of the Germans. She recalled in her autobiography,

> The next morning I went out to view Berlin for the first time. At first I, who had already dreamed of Greece and Greek Art, was momentarily impressed by the architecture of Berlin. [¶] "But this is Greece!" I exclaimed. [¶] But after I examined it more closely I realised that Berlin did not resemble Greece. This was a Nordic impression of Greece. These columns are not the Doric columns which should soar into the skies of Olympian blue. These are the Germanic, pedantic, archaelogical Professors' conception of Greece. And when I saw the Kaiserlich Royal Guard goosestep out of the Doric columns of the Potsdamer Platz, I went home to the Bristol and said, "Geben Sie mir ein Glas Bier. Ich bin müde." (Duncan 1927: 95–96)

Whereas Duncan, during one of her first Munich performances, would be noticed by Siegfried and Cosima Wagner and subsequently invited to dance at Bayreuth, a certain segment of Munich society reacted negatively both to the freedom of her dance and to her use of so-called absolute music as a means to her ends. Eventually, Max Reger entered the fray, siding decidedly with the conservative element against Duncan in what is unquestionably his most creative essay. Although Reger cited the "tone" of the German press as the point of departure for his article, Karl Hasse, who would become Reger's pupil at Munich, claimed that a short protest written by "Frau Prof. Dr. Quidde" — presumably Margarete Quidde (1858–1940), wife of the historian and eventual Nobel Prize winner Ludwig Quidde (1858–1941) — moved Reger to contribute the fantastic fable of his "On April 1" (Hasse 1921: 172). The brevity of Quidde's article,[1] which threatens to lose itself in diatribe, allows for its full reproduction here:

Dear Editors!

> In all of Munich, is there in musical circles really not a single voice to be raised against the unheard-of tomfoolery, the shocking sacrilege, that is to transpire in the Kaim-Saal on Friday evening, the announcements

of which have for days graced enormous posters on all the kiosks? Beethoven … danced! Beethoven's C-sharp-minor Sonata [no. 14, op. 27 no. 2, so-called Moonlight] danced! There is really no protest raised against this in the musical circles of Munich? Instead, all who carry music in their hearts should stand up like men and protest publicly against such a danced, foul desecration, in a way that would simply render impossible such a display, felt to be a shame and disgrace by every serious musician. [¶] That even Beethoven is no longer safe from Ms. Duncan's dance is sad, but it isn't astonishing. That Ms. Duncan lacks artistic sensitivity with respect to music, she has proven once and for all with the impropriety manifested in the production of the "Chopin-Abende." She appears to have no feeling for the fact that musical works of art, born of pure artistic feeling as ends in themselves, are not to be degraded as means to other ends. Why ought she not "dance" the great, holy anguish of a divinely sent figure like Beethoven, since she has already danced Préludes, Nocturnes, etc., at whose creation the composer will have thought of anything but the fact that they ever could be misused by a pair of dance-eager legs? To dance Beethoven is something "new." Perhaps over time, a steady diet of only Chopin and the Renaissance does not exert a powerful attraction upon a public that, after all, quickly becomes bored. Because they caught colds [wegen Verschnupftheit], the Greek boys were sent home to the southern climes, after the complete fiasco experienced by them and the newest mission of Ms. Duncan here and in Berlin.[2] So, from Ms. Duncan's standpoint, Beethoven is at the moment perhaps a quite useful substitute for the cold-ridden Greek boys. [¶] It is not to be expected that the public will protest the production of a Beethoven-Tanz-Abend by staying away, no matter how welcome that would be. In a city where so much Beethoven is performed seriously, the respect paid this great genius would have to run too deep for the public to allow itself an offering of his music as "dance accompaniment." — Everyone knows, by the way, that the public, like a grown child, does not like to let something slip by in which there is a great deal to see — and as is well known, with Ms. Duncan there are all sorts of things to see. But that no protest has ensued from the side of the musicians, that is — despite everything — astonishing and extraordinarily regrettable. As the appointed guardians of the temple, they would have to have voiced their opinion energetically in some way or another. Instead, I understand that a prominent musician here is supposed to have studied the C-sharp-minor Sonata with Ms. Duncan. If that is true, then one certainly need not be any longer surprised at the silence in musical circles. The question then is only: Where are we headed?

Respectfully yours,
Frau M. Quidde (Quidde 1904)

Perhaps as a witty yet earnestly meant answer to Quidde's final question, Reger's essay appeared in the *Neue Zeitschrift* a few weeks later. The story Reger fabricates is in itself simple enough, but the details interlaced throughout are unusually important to the context: on 1 April 1904 — the date of the essay's title — the composer wrote to Karl Straube, "I very much hope that my 'legend of the big toe' will please you — but note: there is deep meaning in the whole!"[3] (Letter of 1 April 1904 in Popp 1986: 52)

On April 1

Dear Editors.

I have just received a very interesting letter, which I permit myself to submit to you below in a word-for-word copy. I ask most respectfully that you do not withhold it from the readers of your very esteemed paper. In view of the constantly growing interest in "bodily worship," or the art of dance respectively [am "körperlichen Gottesdienst" bezw. an der Tanzkunst], the correspondence has become, so to speak, current news.

The letter from my friend of many years reads:

Dear friend!

You will (justifiably!) be very angry with me, and I confess repentantly that I am very embarrassed at having left you so long without news. However, an event that has for weeks held me as if under a spell, and will likely continue to hold sway over me for a long, long time, has prevented me from answering your last letter. — As you know, I usually spend the early months of the year in Nervi,[4] in order to cure my nerves, somewhat devastated by life in the big city, under the eternally laughing heavens of the Riviera. Unfortunately, I did not sense any improvement in Nervi, and so I spent last summer in a small village in the Black Forest, whence I moved in the autumn to Aringsdorf bei Kufstein,[5] acting on the advice of my doctors, in order to take my "solitary cure" (as I call it in jest) in this so delightfully situated little village. You will certainly still remember Aringsdorf, where we met eight years ago,[6] and so it will not surprise you to hear that during the first period of my stay in Aringsdorf, I felt a quickly advancing recuperation of my so assaulted nerves! You, my dear friend, can imagine how very happy I was to learn to forget completely at the breast of nature all the trifles, the superficiality, the blasé — in short, all the "here and there" that life in society brings with it.

There — one day something happened that all at once left my nerves, almost completely cured, in the most dangerous state of agitation thinkable, and my spirit in a state of overexitement that has only grown since the experience. Let me relate it to you! On 21 October I took my usual morning stroll. I encountered Furtler Seppl, whom you will remember from when we attended the delightful Almtanz eight years ago, where he was so devilishly jolly. Seppl, who on this morning (on 21 Oct.)[7] wore an extremely serious face, — *how* rare for Furtler Seppl! — upon my questioning him about his so important secret, took me along to the cow barn of the "Gniseigbauern," whose farm, you perhaps remember, lies a bit outside Aringsdorf beside the "Rasiwirt."

As we (Furtler Seppl and I) entered the cow barn, we encountered a sight that will forever and always remain unforgettable to me, and that will possibly still cost me my senses. I stood before something incomprehensible, gruesome, but at the same time so lovely, lofty, so unspeakably beautiful, that suddenly I was in — Saul's position: "What then actually is beauty!"[8] Listen! Urschl (the milkmaid of the Gniseigbauern), otherwise in normal life rather crude, so to speak, sat upon a wooden stool with eyes shut, her right (of course, naked) foot stretched out horizontally as if in a convulsion. Beside her stood her beau, the Weinbusch Franzl, playing the harmonica, on which he is a virtuoso, as you certainly will still recall. I naturally wanted to question the Weinbusch Franzl — but he signaled to me with vigorous gestures that I should be quiet, and that Urschl's condition was due solely to the effect of music. And now listen! *Urschl was not dancing, moved neither arms nor face*, no, *only her big toe* (of the right foot)! *She had become the purest revelation of the most inner psyche of all art!* I have seen all, all of our famous greater and lesser actors and actresses — but never, ever before has mime moved me to my depths to the extent of this mime, — nay — the utterly elemental expressive power of Urschl's right big toe. More about this later! As you know, eight years ago (as still today) Urschl always walked barefoot. Back then there was nothing extraordinary to notice about Urschl's right big toe: That is to say, eight years ago the two of *us* (you and I) were still far too much caught up in the fatal delusion of so-called good, old art, of absolute music (God bless those who have since that time so gently passed away),[9] that we could have recognized (to speak with Heine) in the enormous significance of this big toe its divine lineage [um eben an der enormen Grösse dieser grossen Zehe (um mit Heine zu reden) deren göttliche Abkunft zu erkennen]! Now listen! The Weinbusch Franzl played the harmonica, and this big toe became the incarnate revelation of the profound, profound, until now mystifying thing that we prosaic people in our paltry language have been wont to designate with the miserable word "beauty." Everything that the Weinbusch Franzl played was transformed by the endlessly elevated, mystical (not manured!) [mystische (nicht mistische!)] mimic and the phenomenal expressive power of this divine big toe. His music became the most moving drama, the most deeply felt experience, the incarnation of the most intimate, unimaginable stirrings of the soul. It was astounding, overwhelming, with what endless, inexhaustible wealth of finest nuance this wonderful right big toe brought to the most vivid, the most convincing expression all of the *differing* sentiments that moved the Weinbusch Franzl's music! But this wasn't enough: This big toe was even able to work miracles! As Franzl played the rustic cow's square dance, a few drops of warm cow's milk flowed — o wonder! — from this big toe. A Soxhlet extractor[10] appeared, hovering from the ceiling, and Franzl, Urschl's beau, grew very quickly a couple of excellent horns. When Franzl then began to play Chopin's Funeral March [Sonata in B-flat minor op. 35] *backward*, I suddenly saw several pale figures, as if resurrected from the dead, flutter over us with grisly, disturbed facial expressions. (Wicked skeptics asserted afterward that these must have been certain beer-saturated corpses who, after some drawn out "eye-opener" pints, had finally started on the way home from the Sariwirt [sic]. I can and must declare this *frightful* assertion as nothing but *vile slander.*)

Now listen further, dear friend! Weinbusch Franzl began to play the C-sharp-minor Fugue of J. S. Bach (Well-Tempered Clavier I) [BWV 849].[11] The wonderful right big toe reared itself in superhuman sovereignty, and grew and grew to unimaginable heights of the most inward expression. Suddenly, in the door of the so prosaic cow barn appeared a figure, aglow in supernatural brilliance, in whose raised right hand — as if in blessing — was held the Gospel of the "inner experience." The figure slowly approached Urschl and touched her right big toe with a little magic wand — the big toe opened up, and — from it emerged the spirit of Joh. Seb. Bach, which spoke: "Oh, thou divine big toe! Now, far from bitter harm, I can take pleasure in the joys of heaven; you have taught me that which was denied me during my earthly pilgrimage, that which, until now, the joys of heaven would repay: Now I finally understand what I wanted to express with my C-sharp-minor Fugue. *Your power of expression, your majesty of transcendental feeling has taught me this.* All praise to you and thanks!" The spirit spoke these words, bowed, and vanished along with the beaming supernatural figure. On the ground, next to the big toe, lay a letter which, I had noticed, had fallen from the pocket of Bach's spirit. I picked up the letter, opened it, and saw to my most gruesome horror the ghostly handwriting of Chopin, who in the most touching, pleading words implored Urschl, or Urschl's right big toe, to redeem him, to help him to find peace in the grave. Since his music had been danced, he had had the most grisly, the most cruel pains. Only the big toe could help him, so that he — that is, his Nocturnos, etc. — was no longer danced. *Only* the transcendental mimic of this big toe could restore his grave's peace. Suddenly, Weinbusch Franzl began to play one of *your* compositions, my dear friend. The big toe reared itself painfully. Urschl opened her eyes, jumped up, and flung the closest milk bucket on my head, whereupon I fled immediately. You can well imagine my astonishment that your music was apparently so unpleasant to this big toe, *you poor thing*!

As I learned later, Urschl in her anger must not have behaved very kindly toward her charges that morning, which brought about the folly of associating these actions with your music; since, from that day forward, Weinbusch Franzl had to refrain completely from playing your compositions, because everytime he tried, such great disquiet arose in the barn.

I've heard from the villagers that Urschl is moonstruck, which I again must declare as underhanded slander. For I have seen with *my* eyes what *no* one before me has ever witnessed. Since that memorable morning, I have become another, happier person. Now I know where to search for true art and the most sublime beauty, and where it is to be found. May the same incomprehensible fortune come to you.

With heartfelt greetings

Your old friend
Ludwig

This is my friend's letter, which I wish the greatest circulation considering its invaluable worth with regard to an appreciation of the essence of art.

Very respectfully yours

Your devoted
Max Reger
Munich, on 1 April 1904

9

Felix Mendelssohn Bartholdy's Songs Without Words

Illustrierte Zeitung Leipzig 3422 (28 January 1909, 152–53)

Introduction

Reger uses this essay, published on the occasion of the one hundredth anniversary of Mendelssohn's birth, not only to discuss the significance of the elder composer's music but also, as he does in essay 7, "Hugo Wolf's Artistic Legacy" of 1904, to disparage the misguided judgment of German critics, audiences, and would-be composers who dismiss

Mendelssohn's music as simplistic in light of Wagner and Liszt. Indeed, Reger had planned the Mendelssohn article as early as 1904 in the wake of the Wolf essay, and when he wrote to his publishers Lauterbach and Kuhn in late January 1904, he clearly linked the two projects in his mind:

> My Hugo Wolf essay has hit home; I'm receiving the most unbelievable communications. Members of a certain Munich camp, or clique, are supposed to be speechless with horror at my article! This doesn't hurt anything! Before long I will write about Felix Mendelssohn! Watch carefully, "that will stir up trouble" ["dös gibt a Hetz"]! (Letter of 28 January 1904 in Müller 1993: 269)

Reger does not develop anything approaching a detailed discussion about the works named in the title; rather, the topic at hand serves as a point of departure for a substantial critique of modern musical culture. It almost need not be said that the essay, which seeks not only to paint Mendelssohn as a composer of "genuinely German music," but also to associate him on a certain level with Richard Wagner, would have been impossible in the German press only some thirty years later.

Because Reger cultivated personal ties with the Mendelssohn family in Leipzig, his relationship to Mendelssohn went beyond a removed interest in the latter's music. Adolf Wach (1843–1926), a legal scholar, university professor, and influential member of the Gewandhaus board, had taken an interest in Reger's music and became instrumental in the latter's Leipzig appointments in 1907. Wach was wed to Lili Mendelssohn Bartholdy (1845–1912), youngest daughter of the composer, to whose memory Reger would dedicate his motet *O Tod, wie bitter bist du* op. 110 no. 3 (see Figure 9.1). Further, during his last years, Reger frequented the home of the Leipzig banker Ludwig Mendelssohn Bartholdy, the composer's grandson, and his wife Edith (1882–1969), who cultivated a lively appreciation for Reger's music and published a brief but engaging reminiscence of him in 1956 (Mendelssohn Bartholdy 1956).

Felix Mendelssohn Bartholdy's Songs Without Words

My readers should not fear that I, following the trend of our time, am going to give a thorough technical analysis of the *Songs Without Words.*

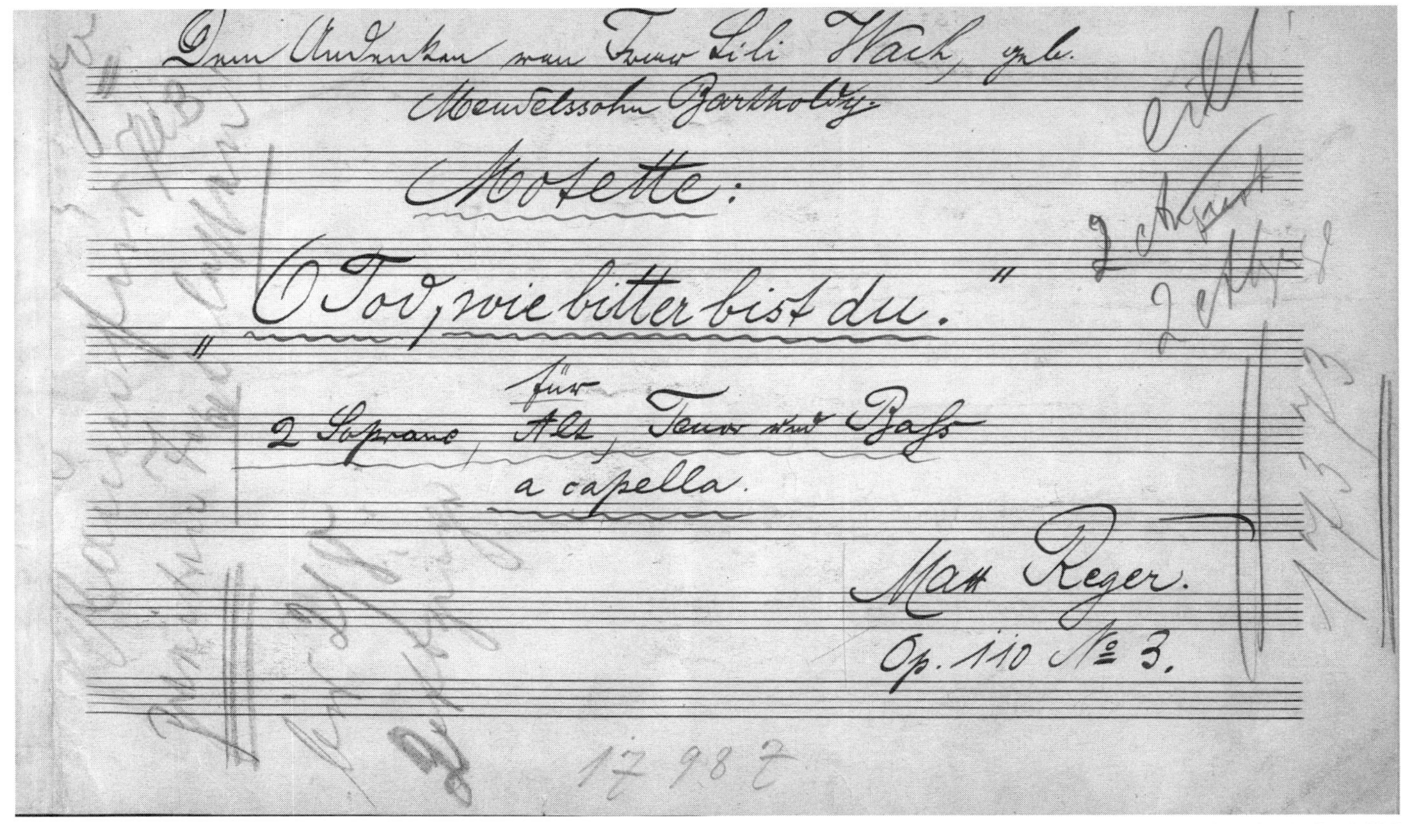

Figure 9.1 Max Reger: "Motet O Tod, wie bitter bist du" op. 110 no. 3, autograph page 1, with dedication "To the memory of Frau Lili Wach, born Mendelssohn Bartholdy" (1912).

Such things are just as edifying as they are delightful to read: They almost always betray infinite acumen but usually amount to wasted effort [verlorene Liebesmüh].[1] The point of the present essay is only to call express attention to a portion of Mendelssohn's oeuvre that seems to have disappeared in our busy modern musical culture. Anyone for whom treble and bass clef as well as some knowledge of the keyboard is not a "Bohemian village" knows what huge popularity and wide circulation the *Songs Without Words* enjoyed a few decades ago. Of course the enormous "revaluation" of all music occasioned by Wagner and Liszt at first forced the most distinguished representatives of refined formal architecture into the background, and, in the ebb and flow of time, we have seen that such a sensitive, warm-hearted, great master as Mendelssohn has been and continues to be almost forgotten, or in any case completely undervalued — and this after the period in which even a Robert Schumann appeared horribly formless and confused to the dear Germans, always so unrefined in artistic matters, and Mendelssohn was justifiably praised as the zenith of musical development in his time. In order to point out the complete error — not to say obstinancy — of the views of those who react to Mendelssohn with only a pitying smile, I should state here briefly that, since organ music had sunk into a deep slumber after Bach, it was Mendelssohn's organ sonatas that appeared as the most prominent [markanteste] new repertory nearly a hundred years after Bach's death.[2] Those who know how much organ music was composed during the period between Bach and Mendelssohn are able more nearly to judge what "great deeds" Mendelssohn's organ works are. Furthermore, the musical world possesses in the overtures to *Midsummer Night's Dream* and *The Hebrides* such precious jewels of genuinely German music, such shining examples of warm-hearted, refined art that confer immortality on their creator.[3]

It is true that such a towering figure as Mendelssohn immediately found countless imitators who could not be satisfied to follow in the master's footsteps without actually becoming a "second Mendelssohn" — thereby bringing about a serious leveling of the style and the ideas expressed by it.[4] In the same way, the "spiritual slaves" of the greatest dramatic genius of all time, Richard Wagner, will not be able to create anything more lasting than Mendelssohn's imitators. Perhaps it will surprise some of my associates that I so readily turn my attention to Mendelssohn and that I very often play his *Songs Without Words*.[5] Perhaps I am regarded as a "retrogressive in disguise," or perhaps certain people rejoice that I now have finally renounced my chromatic madness and other "alarming" things, free harmony, unbridled tonality — whatever one would like to call my unforgivable crimes against "noble," "true" art; that is, against the kind of art loved by those who so thoroughly dislike having their peace disturbed when listening to music.

What is so attractive to me about Mendelssohn is the truth of expression, the honesty of sentiment that permeates the artistic as well as personal essence of a thoroughly distinguished artist. Particularly in the *Songs Without Words*, such perfect use of the piano's technical possibilities and such absolute command of the musical and formal material are evident that we can only prescribe most urgently a thorough bath in Mendelssohn to all those confused and errant young *Übermenschen*, for whom music begins only with an eighth horn, with four woodwinds of a kind, with 64 percussion instruments, and several dozen differently tuned bells. In our day, one laments that the noble practice of domestic music making threatens to die out.[6] This would be the time to return the *Songs Without Words* to a position of honor, if only one could realize that music can be enjoyed without the pomp of modern concert halls, without the flaunting of the latest trends. To reach this goal — the reintroduction of the *Songs Without Words* into domestic settings — requires the cooperation of those who play a significant role in public musical life as performing artists or critics. Unfortunately, I must say that the press as well as the latest "hothead" composers have often sinned greatly in this respect. I know certain "heroes" of the press, as well as some young "prophets" afflicted with a grave misunderstanding of Wagner and Liszt, who scornfully turn up their noses at Mendelssohn. Furthermore, I am acquainted with these gentlemen on a very exact basis and know only too well that the actual ability, the compositional talents of these "wannabes" taken all together will never suffice to produce even one work of the quality and workmanship of a *Song Without Words*.

Is it really no longer possible that a sensitive pianist — one whose ideal does not lie with the development of the most robust touch[7] — can earn some recognition for poetic performances of Mendelssohn's piano works? Did not so eminent an artist as Bülow have the greatest esteem for Mendelssohn, and did he not perform Mendelssohn well into his late years?[8] And surely no one would accuse Bülow, who always fought in the front ranks of progress, of "backwardness" with respect to his insight or quality of judgment! Bülow's most basic motto — "Honor your German masters"[9] — obligates us, too, to honor forever the great, German master Felix Mendelssohn.

Reger

10

[On Johann Sebastian Bach]

Die Musik 5/1 (October 1905): 74

Introduction

In 1905, the periodical *Die Musik* issued a questionnaire to artists, teachers, writers, and scholars inside and outside of Germany, requesting responses to the question "What is Johann Sebastian Bach to me, and what does he mean to our time?" ["Was ist mir Johann Sebastian Bach und was bedeutet er für unsere Zeit?"] The result was a collection of eighty-seven replies, some of them brief, others of essay proportions complete with footnotes and musical examples, which take up the entire issue of October 1905. Reger's answer, among the shortest, appears as number 82. According to a detailed *Vorbemerkung*, the responses were organized by age of the respondents, oldest to youngest. The brevity of Reger's "essay," however, does not prevent the emergence of certain themes that are developed at greater length elsewhere in his writings: the nature of progress, the "illness" of contemporary musical culture, German nationalism, the guilt of the critics.

On Johann Sebastian Bach

For me, Seb. Bach is the beginning and end of all music. *All true* progress is based on and rests with him!

What Seb. Bach means — pardon — *ought* to mean for our time?

A most powerful and inexhaustible remedy not only for all those composers and performers who have become ill from "misunderstood Wagner," but also for all those "contemporaries" who suffer from spinal atrophy [Rückenmarkschwindsucht] of all kinds. To be "Bachian" means to be *proto-Germanic, unyielding.*

That Bach could be misjudged for so long is the *greatest disgrace* for the "*critical* wisdom" of the eighteenth and nineteenth centuries.

11

[On Richard Strauss]

Allgemeine Musik-Zeitung 39/43 (October 1912): 1070; and *Der Merker* 5/112 (May 1914): 394

Introduction

In October 1912, the *Allgemeine Musik-Zeitung* published a set of 32 responses to the question "In your opinion, wherein lies the actual significance of Richard Strauss's works thus far for musical development after Wagner and Liszt?" ["Worin liegt nach Ihrer Meinung die eigentliche Bedeutung von Richard Strauß' bisherigem Schaffen für die musikalische Fortentwickelung nach Wagner und Liszt?"] Reger's answer (no. 22) is not only one of the two most succinct (rivaled only by Otto Neitzel's "*In progress*" ["*Im Fortschritt*"]), but he was also the only respondent to sign with his last name only (signatures are reproduced as such rather than typeset; Reger does the same at the end of essay 9): This suggests his thinking about the nature of his own position as a composer, certainly equal to that of Strauss, whose full name he gives with that of Franz Liszt. No doubt significantly, Reger avoids one of the cues in the question by not mentioning Wagner.

The second statement appeared in 1914, written while Reger was recuperating at Meran from the last of his serious nervous breakdowns. In observance of Strauss's fiftieth birthday, the Austrian paper *Der Merker* published a set of six essays in May 1914, authored by Richard Specht, Hermann Bahr, Leopold Schmidt, Siegmund von Hausegger, Arthur Seidl, and Richard Mandl. Reger's statement is appended unobtrusively and without title at the end of the last essay (Mandl's "Meine Begegnung mit Richard Strauss"). Reger's portrayal of Strauss as a "thoroughly classical figure" might usefully be read against the younger composer's much more extensive musical tribute to Strauss at fifty, the Fantasy and Fugue in D minor op. 135b for organ, dedicated to "Meister Richard Strauß in besonderer Verehrung" and composed between 1914 and 1916.

1. On Richard Strauss (1912)

For me, Richard Strauss is the brilliant consummation of the art for which a Franz Liszt has paved the way.

Reger

2. On Richard Strauss (1914)

In the bustle of our musical era, blinded by an insane "process of disintegration," Dr. Richard Strauss is a thoroughly classical figure of the most solid ability — and once more, ability.

Meran, 25 April 1914
Max Reger

Part IV
"Analyses" of Reger's Works for the Festivals of the Allgemeiner Deutscher Musikverein

12

STRING QUARTET OP. 74 IN D MINOR

Die Musik 3/16 (May 1904): 244–47

Introduction

Composed at the beginning of 1904, Reger's String Quartet in D minor op. 74 was to be the third of five quartets assigned opus numbers in his oeuvre (no. 1 in G minor op. 54 and no. 2 in A major op. 54 issue from the end of 1900 and the beginning of 1901, respectively; no. 4 in E-flat major op. 109 appeared in 1909; and no. 5 in F-sharp minor op. 121 was composed in 1911). It revisits the key of a youthful D-minor quartet (without opus number) Reger composed early in 1889. The monumental quartet op. 74, which requires the better part of an hour to perform, issues from one of the most fecund periods of Reger's creative life, a time that fostered the equally adventuresome *Gesang der Verklärten* for chorus and orchestra op. 71, the Violin Sonata in C major op. 72, and the *Variations and Fugue on an Original Theme* for organ op. 73. The mammoth proportions, experimental stance toward thematic coherence, harmonic complexity, and sustained chromaticism within a tonal framework are characteristic of his major works around this time.

Reger submitted the following analysis of the Quartet op. 74 for inclusion in the program book for the May 1904 Tonkünstlerfest of the Allgemeiner Deutscher Musikverein in Frankfurt am Main, at which the work was to be premiered by the Frankfurt Museum Quartet. As it happened, that performance was cancelled at the last minute due to the illness of the violist Fritz Bassermann, with Reger's Violin Sonata op. 72 offered as a substitute on 31 May. Due to the change of program, Reger was able to prove his point, so often expressed in his essays, about the scandalous blunders of the critics: not realizing that op. 72, rather than op. 74, would be performed, several (eight, according to Reger himself) German papers published reviews of the performance of op. 74, obviously written before the work was premiered, presumably using Reger's analysis as raw material (postcard of 11 June 1904 to Carl Lauterbach and Max Kuhn in Müller 1993: 328).

Of the essays included in part IV of the present volume, Reger's discussion of the Quartet op. 74 is both the earliest and the only one that even approaches a standard analysis. Even here, his satirical tone and dry wit waste little time in coming to the surface, and he subsequently abandoned any attempt to treat his works in the critical, academic fashion then current.[1] Asked later that same year to supply analyses of the Violin Sonata op. 72, the String Trio in A minor op. 77b, and the *Variations and Fugue on a Theme of Beethoven* for two pianos op. 86, he wrote to Walter Fischer:

> "Now I am supposed to write analyses for you of opp. 72, 77b and 86 — my dear, I *cannot* do this; it is for me an *impossible* thing to supply analyses of my own works. You can do this much better than I; play *through* this music for yourself and simply write down your opinion of it — that's the best way!" (Letter of 5 December 1904 in Schreiber 1956: 155)

When Karl Straube had asked Reger earlier in 1904 to say something about his organ variations op. 73 (dedicated to Straube), he pointed only generally to the "quite melancholy tone" ["recht wehmütigen Stimmung"] of the whole and the importance of the theme's third bar: "I believe that will surely suffice. You know that I so terribly dislike speaking about it, because I perceive it as a 'pose' to 'show off' ['protzen'] with one's own moods and sentiments" (letter of 25 June 1904 in Popp 1986: 58). Regardless of this way of thinking, though, the composer certainly does not suppress his personality in this discussion, and in the subsequent "analyses," he allows it complete freedom.

Reger does not distinguish musical passages by measure numbers. When it has appeared helpful, I have included these, as well as indications of instrumentation, in brackets.

String Quartet op. 74 in D minor

The work has four movements. The *first movement* in 6/8, Allegro agitato e vivace, commences with the following principal theme, played by the four strings in unison:

[I/1–5, vln. 2]

This theme is followed immediately by a new, frequently recurring motive:

etc.

[I/6, vln. 1]

The musical language becomes more and more agitated, leading to the emergence of the following new motive:

etc.

[I/27, vln. 1]

This theme receives a striking harmonization and leads to the reappearance of the principal theme (in D minor and F-sharp minor) in free imitation between violin 1 and the violoncello. After a short pianissimo episode:

etc.

[I/34–35, vln. 1][2]

and after an increasingly passionate development by way of some new motives, the insistent appearance of the principal theme, and stammering syncopations (violin 2 and viola [I/82–90]), the true second theme of the first movement appears in F major:

score page 6

[I/91–95, vln. 1]

By way of a sharply dissonant B-flat in the first violin [I/120] issues directly the extremely agitated closing group, consisting of familiar as well as new thematic material. The principal theme of the whole movement appears in rude exchange with the other themes in inversion and diminution. This molto agitato comes to a sudden halt, giving way to a songlike statement of the first violin (con sordino) supported by sustained harmony [I/139]. After this pianissimo episode comes a new motive and an intensification of the principal theme, which gradually dissolves into the quiet harmony of the second theme. Sustained F-major chords close the exposition.

The development begins immediately with a new theme (violin 1) in D major, supported by the tranquil harmony of the other instruments [I/178]. The sudden emergence of the principal themes incites an intensification to agitato. Again, quieter episodes appear (formed partially from the principal theme) after transitional pizzicati of the violoncello. A short, passionate violoncello solo [I/223] leads to very lively development of the previously introduced themes, sometimes in rather rude exchange. The waves calm; the hesitant syncopations from the exposition's transition to the second theme lead to the second theme itself, now with substantially new harmony [I/246].

After a short intensification and marked exchange between ff and p

(NB. the first interval of the second theme [I/266, vln. 1])

develops a most innocent fugato formed from the first six notes of the principal theme [I/271].

After several combinations of the two principal themes, and after a short, energetic intensification, the recapitulation commences [I/315], introduced by a poco meno mosso and ppp. After the recapitulation, which presents the exposition with very few changes, and after the sustained D-major chords, the short coda begins [I/423], freely juxtaposing the first principal theme and the second theme, bringing the first movement to a close in a stormy fff.

The *following* Vivace in C major 2/4 stands in the greatest possible contrast to the turbulent language of the first movement. The "very cheerful" ["kreuzfidel"] theme is:

[II/1–4, vln. 1, 2, vla.]

Eventually appear here and there some smaller themes which function rather ironically. Nevertheless, all of them are immediately comprehensible to everyone who is even somewhat musical, and who does not detect a perverse musical vein of the composer behind every ♮ and ♭. After a short, melancholy transition in C-sharp minor [II/147–64] — please forgive the key progression of C major to C-sharp minor and back again — the nightmare begins all over again, but now the various themes are introduced in an order different from that of the opening. A more and more frenzied mischievousness contents itself in the end with innocent pizzicati — and bids adieu.

The *third movement*, Andante sostenuto e semplice, has the following theme:

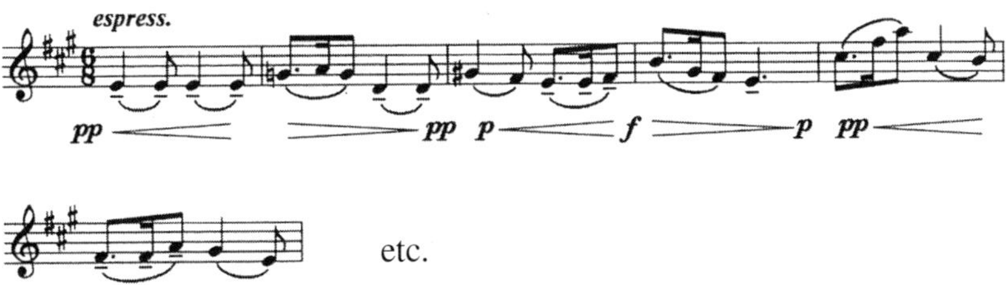

etc.

[III/1–6, vln. 1]

Following this simple theme is a series of eleven variations in A major (variations 1–5), in D major (variation 6), in D minor (variation 7), in F-sharp minor (variation 8) with a transition (variation 9) to A minor (variation 10), and in A major (variation 11).

The *fourth movement*, primarily of a cheerful character, has the following theme:

[IV/1–5, vln.1]

After the repetition of this theme fortissimo (following new transitional motives), a new theme appears, which later plays an important role in this movement:

[IV/34–35, vln. 1][3]

A more extended transition leads to the second theme, which exhibits a purposeful similarity to the second theme of the first movement:

etc.

[IV/69–71, vln. 1]

I give one further small theme, later employed frequently:

[IV/88–89, vln. 1]

After the ensuing reprise of the first theme, the third theme in A minor emerges:

[IV/122–26, vln. 1][4]

and

[IV/126–27, vla., cello][5]

Then commences the development, in which all these themes are juxtaposed in the most free, capricious manner. A further, energetic appearance of the third theme leads — after various mischievous gestures, apparent fugatos, and similar "austere masks" — to D major, back to the first theme of the rondo [IV/334]. Except in only a few bars, the reprise of the first portion of the rondo is conceived predictably. A brief coda [IV/458] (from the principal theme), perhaps alarming to timid and immature dispositions, brings the closing rondo to an end. I emphasize that my String Quartet op. 74 involves no hidden or "forswearable" program. The work desires merely to be music.[6] The listener is free to imagine something with respect to it, if desired.

Max Reger

13

Variations and Fugue on a Theme of Joh. Seb. Bach for Piano, Two Hands op. 81; and Variations and Fugue on a Theme of Beethoven for Two Pianos, Four Hands op. 86

Die Musik 4/17 (June 1905): 316–17

Introduction

In June 1905, the Allgemeiner Deutscher Musikverein held its Tonkünstlerfest at Graz, where Reger's piano works opp. 81 and 86 received performances. Unlike for the festival of the previous year, and perhaps in reaction to the fiasco of his op. 74 quartet having been reviewed before it was heard (see essay 12), Reger here merely announces the principal themes of opp. 81 and 86,[1] closing what might fairly be called his "anti-analysis" with a typically sarcastic warning about the harmlessness of chromaticism.[2] The self-conferred title of "note writer" speaks to the often-voiced criticism of Reger as an overly prolific mere technician with no control over his muse.

1. Variations and Fugue on a Theme of Joh. Seb. Bach for Piano, Two Hands op. 81

Beginning of the theme:

First fugue theme:

Second fugue theme:

2. Variations and Fugue on a Theme of Beethoven for Two Pianos, Four Hands op. 86

Beginning of the theme:

etc.

Theme of the fugue:

Everything else that "transpires" ["passiert"] in this music is immediately clear and comprehensible to anyone who is not scared of "a few" ♮, ♭, ♯, X, ♮♭, ♭♭, and ♮♯.

Max Reger
German note writer [Deutscher Notenschreiber]

14

Psalm 100 for Chorus, Orchestra, and Organ op. 106

Die Musik 9/16 (May 1910): 225

Introduction

Psalm 100 was a gift to the University of Jena upon its granting Reger an honorary Ph.D. degree in the summer of 1908. Reger composed the first of op. 106's four movements in 1908, completing the work in 1909 and leading its full premiere in February 1910. The piece was given another performance on 27 May 1910, at the festival of the Allgemeiner

Deutscher Musikverein in Zurich. As with op. 74 at the 1904 festival, and with opp. 81 and 86 at the 1905 festival, Reger prepared an "analysis" of op. 106 for the program booklet, removed more than ever from any sort of serious discussion. Whereas in 1905 (essay 13) he had followed convention by merely quoting the main themes of opp. 81 and 86, here Reger invents a mock pseudotheme in 7/4 time, saturated with impossible chromaticism (note the triple-sharped c^2 as the sixth tone).

Psalm 100

The words of the psalm will be familiar to anyone who does not maintain a harem. Whether or not my setting of this psalm contains themes, I do not know: I will be advised in this regard by the critics. I have held *absolutely strictly* to the key of D major. It is said that the psalm is organized in three sections: The listener is accordingly warned of a few very nasty pedal points. The principal theme of the whole work, perhaps occasionally audible, is:

Max Reger

15

Quartet for Violin, Viola, Violoncello, and Piano op. 113

Die Musik 9/16 (May 1910): 248–49

Introduction

Reger's Quartet in D minor op. 113 was composed in April 1910 and given its premiere from the manuscript on 30 May of that year at the forty-sixth composers' festival of the Allgemeiner Deutscher Musikverein in Zurich, the same gathering at which *Psalm 100* op. 106 was performed, and for which Reger supplied the satirical comments of essay 14. Joining Reger at the piano were Willem de Boer, Joseph Ebner, and Engelbert Röntgen, all members of the Zurich String Quartet. Again underscoring the folly of those who expect to take away something essential from program-note criticism, the composer offers the following self-deprecating discussion, completely free of thematic citation, and typical of his wit.

Quartet for Violin, Viola, Violoncello, and Piano op. 113

The work has of course four movements, which fact is founded in my penchant for musical discursiveness. The Larghetto (third movement) goes rather slowly; according to established custom, one of course ought to take the other three movements more quickly. But with this work one could do it the other way around — the music will sound terrible in either case. The key is D minor — for which extremely bold assertion I can assume no responsibility. It is pointless to reproduce the themes here, since they really never can be heard. A revered musical police is hereby notified of the fact that in precisely this work — as unfortunately quite often — I have plagiarized to an appalling degree. Interestingly enough, however, I have refrained from fugues [Fugen] and other such mischief [Unfug].

Max Reger

P. S. Should the harmony prove to be not always bacteria-free, I ask all apostles of tonal chastity for forgiveness.

16

Römischer Triumphgesang for Men's Chorus and Orchestra op. 126

Die Musik 12/17 (June 1913): 301

Introduction

The occasion for Reger's pompous op. 126 — *Römischer Triumphgesang* (text by the German poet Hermann Lingg) for four-part men's chorus and orchestra — was, as with his *Psalm 100* op. 106, the awarding of an honorary doctorate, an M.D. from the medical faculty of the Friedrich-Wilhelm University of Berlin, to whom op. 126 is dedicated. The work received its premiere on 6 June 1913 at the Tonkünstlerfest of the Allgemeiner Deutscher Musikverein, held that year in Jena. Despite what Reger's ultraminimalist "analysis" might suggest, the work is disposed in a single movement cast in E-flat major. The "themes" given here are of course entirely fictional, and it is appropriate that the "essay" that delivers them closes this volume, since it actually may be seen to represent the composer's most radical statement about the impotence of critical writing. Reger's submission prompted a note by the editor of *Die Musik*, who, instead of publishing a portrait of Reger (as with the other twenty-four composers whose music was heard at the festival), offered instead three recently completed caricatures by Wilhelm Thielmann.

Römischer Triumphgesang for Men's Chorus and Orchestra p. 126

*Max Reger**

* As is well known, Max Reger has a sense of humor. He will therefore not be surprised that we publish, instead of a "correct" portrait, a few caricatures of him in the pictorial portion of this issue. This is our revenge for his witty "analysis"! (The Editor)

Notes

Introduction: Max Reger and the Written Word

1. The formulation paraphrases an observation of Carl Dahlhaus in his brief essay for the Reger anniversary year 1973, "Warum ist Regers Musik so schwer verständlich?" (Dahlhaus 1973).
2. It must certainly be true that the existing autograph, shown as Figure 7.1 and discussed further below and in the commentary to essay 7, is the final draft copy of an even earlier version of the Wolf essay, now lost.
3. On Reger's Meiningen practices, which transpose the tendencies discussed here to the arenas of musical analysis, rehearsal, and performance, see Anderson 2004b.
4. It is impossible not to wonder whether the seemingly arbitrary opus number is significant in some way, and whether, if this is so, it should be read "32571," i.e., backward, like the rest of the piece.
5. Reger's striving toward "healthy music" parallels his habitual insistence, made to various correspondents throughout his life, that he himself remained "kerngesund," or "healthy to the core," able to bear the weight of an enormous workload out of reach for most people.
6. A facsimile of the autograph appears in Popp 1986: 15. Note that the remark parallels the "analysis" of op. 113 by calling not only on the idea of health (the "bacteria-ridden" music of op. 113, the "deaths" associated with listening to op. 52 no. 1) — i.e., it is dangerous to listen to Reger's music — but also on the notion of crime (the "police" in the remarks about op. 113, the "crime" of op. 52 no. 1) — i.e., it is wrong to compose in Reger's style.
7. See the discussion that accompanies essay 2, "More Light."

1. I Request the Floor!

1. Reger's disdain for so-called *innere Erlebnisse* manifests itself often in these essays. See further the introduction to this volume.
2. In a letter of 8 February 1904 to Karl Straube, Reger made clear that "I Request the Floor!" was his answer to Smolian's criticism. His comment there, "Soon will ensue the execution of 2 gentlemen [in Bälde kommt die Hinrichtung von 2 Herren]" (Popp 1986: 50), presumably refers to Smolian and Max Arend: the latter is the author of the criticism which Reger answers in essay 2, "More Light." See also Reger's assessment of both Smolian and Arend in a letter of 7 April 1904 to Carl Lauterbach and Max Kuhn in Müller 1993: 124.
3. In his reprinting of Reger's essays, Karl Hasse had pointed out that this phrase, cited again by Reger in the essay below, is drawn from Goethe's *Faust* II (Hasse 1921: 160). The relevant passage is an exclamation of Ariel at the arrival of dawn in Act I: "Horchet! horcht dem Sturm der Horen!/Tönend wird für Geistesohren/Schon der neue Tag geboren."
4. Reger had been given duties as a theory instructor at the Wiesbaden Conservatory as early as 1890, while still a pupil of Hugo Riemann. See Reger's letter of 16 November 1890 to Adalbert Lindner in Popp 2000: 80. In 1905, he would receive an appointment at the Munich Akademie der Tonkunst as an instructor in counterpoint, succeeding Josef Rheinberger. From 1907, Reger taught theory and composition at the Leipzig Conservatory.
5. It is perhaps worth noting that Reger himself had not been spared discussions of his music that turned precisely on the rhetorical antithesis of "das Musikalisch-Schöne" (here, certainly an allusion to Eduard Hanslick's *Vom musikalisch Schönen*) and "das Musikalisch-Hässliche," the most well known of which may be Rudolf Louis's acerbic review, written less than a year before the present essay, of a performance of the *Symphonic Fantasy and Fugue* op. 57 for organ, in which he denounced Reger's music as belonging to a "cult of ugliness for its own sake [… Kult des Häßlichen um seiner selbst willen]." The original review appears in the *Münchner Neueste Nachrichten* of 23 June 1903 and is reproduced in Schreiber 1981b: 34–35.
6. Reger's analysis of this modulation (not reproduced in the essay itself) is typical of the treatise: "Tonika C-dur; Oberdominante (G-dur) von C-dur; Umdeutung dieses G-dur zur Unterdominante in D-dur, welches D-dur (als Sextaccord gesetzt) als Accord der neapolitanischen Sexte (fis a d) von cis-moll aufgefasst wird. (Cadenz!)" (Reger 1903: 17)

7. In the example at hand (the modulation from C major to C-sharp minor; see the analysis in note 6 above), Reger reinterprets the first-inversion D-major chord on beat three as the Neapolitan of C-sharp minor, but the Neapolitan itself may be seen as the minor subdominant of C-sharp (major or minor, i.e., F-sharp minor) with a substituted sixth, or, in Reger's language, with an unresolved suspension on D. See further the discussion of this issue in his defense of the *Beiträge* against the objections of Max Arend in essay 2, "More Light." Also, Reger follows Riemann and others in referring to the "sub-" as well as "superdominant," (*Unterdominante*, *Oberdominante*), a nonmenclature that reflects the symmetry of these two harmonies around the tonic, and I have retained that language here. (Bernhoff translates "Oberdominante" as "dominant" in his English edition of the *Beiträge Reger 1904e*.)
8. The turn of phrase recalls Christ's Sermon on the Mount as recorded in Matthew 5:3 ("Blessed are the poor in spirit; for theirs is the kingdom of heaven").
9. It is clear from Reger's subsequent correspondence that he had hoped for a public rejoinder from Smolian, to which he planned a second essay in reply. A new article by Smolian was not forthcoming, though, and the "Smolian affair" died with the present essay, despite Reger's plans to drive the controversy to an invidious head.

2. "More Light"

1. Arend writes, "Daß gerade *Reger*, der sich als kühner Neuerer auf dem Gebiete der Kammermusik schnell einen Namen errungen hat, dazu berufen ist, dieses Praktikum der Theorie seines Lehrers *Riemann* zu liefern, kann keinem Zweifel unterliegen" (Arend 1903–4a: 78).
2. Richter's and Helm's "tried and true" works were in general circulation well before Riemann's. Ernst Friedrich Richter (1808–79) taught at the Leipzig Conservatory and is the author of several texts on harmonic and contrapuntal theory which, because of their uncomplicated language and succinct style, achieved popularity among students in Reger's time. See for example Richter's *Lehrbuch der Harmonie: Praktische Anleitung zu den Studien in derselben* (Richter 1853). In addition, Reger here refers presumably to Johann Helm's (1842–1917) *Allgemeine Musik- und Harmonielehre* (Helm 1870), which in 1911 he would recommend as "vorzüglich" for the studies of Ralf Freiherr von Saalfeld, grandson to Georg II of Sachsen-Meiningen. See Reger's letter of 31 December 1911 in Mueller von Asow 1949: 78–79.

3. Riemann's functional harmonic theory is built entirely around the symmetrical relationship of the tonic triad to the (super)dominant above and subdominant below, a symmetry further reflected in the dualism of the major and minor triad. According to Riemann, the major triad (indicated by the superscript $^{+}$) justifies itself from the overtone series and, consequently, is conceived from the bottom (root) up. The minor triad (indicated by the superscript$^{\circ}$) expresses the opposite principle, justified by resultant tones and conceived from the top down. Therefore, the A-major triad in Riemann's system is designated as "a^{+}," whereas the A-minor triad is calculated from the fifth down, hence "unter-E" or "$^{\circ}$e." The basics of Riemann's system, at once simple and complex, are outlined in several sources, but perhaps the most pertinent to the present context is Gerd Sievers' *Die Grundlagen Hugo Riemanns bei Max Reger* (Sievers 1967).
4. The basis of Arend's argument is his claim that the ear cannot accept the B-sharp major triad on beat 4 as such, rather only as a return to C major, "because for the time being it does not know what to make of the F-sharp major triad [weil es vorläufig noch nicht weiß, was es mit dem Fisdur-Akkord machen soll]" on beat 3, appearing as it does between identical harmonies, regardless of enharmonic spelling (Arend 1903–4a: 79).
5. Riemann had adopted Oettingen's language to describe harmonic movement, later rejected by him as unneccesarily cumbersome, and noticeably absent from the Arend–Reger exchange. In his *Musikalische Syntaxis: Grundriss einer harmonischen Satzbildungslehre*, Riemann discusses movement from a major or minor chord to a harmony of like (homonom) or opposite (antinom) quality, and movement in the same (homolog) or opposite (antilog) direction of the originating harmony: for the major triad, then, conceived upward from the root, the "homolog" direction is upwards, the "antilog" downwards; for the minor triad, conceived downwards from the fifth, the "homolog" direction is downwards, the "antilog" upward. Concerning the issue at hand, Riemann asserted, "The homonom, as well as the antilog-antinom progression of the system's augmented fourth, and the antilog-antinom progressions by leading tone, third, and sixth, find their place at most once in development sections. They are not appropriate placed next to one another in the construction of themes, rather they require further continuous [harmonic] explanation" (Riemann 1877: 98).
6. Example 33 demonstrated the modulation from C major to G minor, whereas example 56 showed a similar movement from A minor to G

minor. The second printing also integrated the analyses with the examples, rather than separating them at the back of the volume.

7. Reger has not given here exactly what had been printed in Arend's discussion. That example had, as Reger suggests, contained a printing error on the second chord of the second bar:

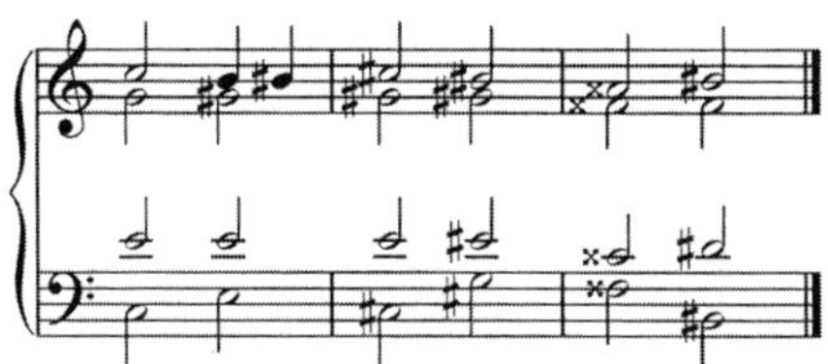

Obviously, Arend did not intend an E-sharp minor 6-chord and the ensuing parallel octave, but rather, as the printed accidental suggests, a root-position triad. Arend pointed this out in his published reply to Reger's essay (see below). Further, Arend had referred to the second chord in the first bar of his example as F major rather than E major.

8. Reger alludes of course to the *Denkmäler deutscher Tonkunst*, launched in 1892 by a committee that included Brahms, Joachim, and Spitta, among others. By the time of Reger's writing, the series had achieved fourteen volumes of music by old masters, including Scheidt, Buxtehude, Kuhnau, and Hassler. In Reger's eyes, the *Denkmäler* undoubtedly represented the double-edged sword of Musikwissenschaft, whereby a healthy interest in old music was clouded by a Beckmesser-like pedantry that in turn determined the tone of contemporary criticism.

9. Arend published a reply to Reger (Arend 1903–4b) in which he states that, despite the correction in the second printing of minor errors in the *Beiträge*, "… the essence of my assessment remains untouched, namely that *Reger* does not always take care to ensure that the ear has the occasion, or even the possibility, of *realising* the functional progression of chords *thought out* by the author, that he therefore pursues a kind of extramusical mathematics of the mind and does harm to the principles of modulation, since the latter must *compel* the listener. If nevertheless the second printing is to be mentioned here, then I should take the opportunity to point out the great success with which *Reger*'s work has been met in the marketplace, which is in any case not undeserved" (Arend 1903–4b). Arend does take time to answer Reger's points, though, since the latter " … in his anti-review surely is thinking only of the reader who, from lack of educational background, cannot follow him and therefore concurs with the opinion of the one who — talks the loudest" (ibid.).

3. Music and Progress

1. L. J. Lawrence has translated the essay as "Is There an Avant-Garde in Music?" but in order to retain the political overtones inherent in the German term, I have translated "Fortschrittspartei" as "progressive party" throughout. Otherwise, I have used Lawrence's translation in citing the essay. Draeseke's and Strauss's articles, as well the four pieces given here in Part II as essays 3–6, are reproduced in Shigihara 1990. The reader is referred especially to Shigihara's (Introduction 1–37) for further background regarding the Draeseke affair.
2. "Professional musicians, anxiously concerned as they are for their own position, artistically impotent, possessing only a certain musical technique culled from some artistic epoch of the past, stubbornly and violently opposed to all expansion of means of expression and artistic form, and critics whose views of art are based on the petrified aesthetics of the past, are once again stirring abroad as a united 'Reactionary Party' endeavouring more than ever to make things difficult for those who wish to go forward" (Strauss 1907: 15).
3. On Reger's attitude about the position of new music in conservatory curricula, see further essay 4, "An Open Letter," especially note 19.
4. Reger must be referring to the passage in Strauss's essay in which the latter mentions the positive judgment of the public versus the negative one of the critics "approximately fifty years ago" to Liszt's symphonic poems (Strauss 1907: 14–15). Whereas Strauss here tries to demonstrate the superiority of the mass's reaction, Reger's point is that the prevalent critical narrow-mindedness proves its own worthlessness by contradicting itself.
5. Strauss's rejection was for Reger the most glaring confirmation of the establishment's heinous backwardness, and he returns to it at the end of essay 4. The Berlin Akademie der Künste would elect Strauss to its membership in 1909.
6. Reger calls on the names of Friedrich Brandes and Friedrich Spiro, neither of whom were inclined to accept the musical language of Strauss or Reger, as a way to draw an ideological bridge between himself and the older composer. Such a link ran counter to the popular image of the two as leaders of opposing camps. Brandes (1864–1940) was a composer, conductor, and editor who had been a pupil of Spitta and Kretzschmar; Spiro (1863–?) was a scholar and critic active in Germany and Italy.
7. Lawrence translates this as "Not for us all those things whose existence is justified solely by the fact that they existed yesterday" (Strauss 1907: 16–17).

8. For a somewhat expanded defense of Brahms along the same lines, see the answer to Hugo Riemann in essay 6, "Degeneration and Regeneration in Music." Lukas Haselböck has recently pointed out that Reger's image of Brahms as a progressive artist anticipates Arnold Schoenberg's attitude in the well-known essay "Brahms the Progressive" (Haselböck 2000: 15–26).
9. The question of ability (*Können*) is, like its conceptual opposite "das innere Erlebnis," a favorite theme that returns leitmotiv-like throughout these essays. See the introduction to this volume.
10. Periodically throughout his career, Reger articulated his attitude about the relevance of the past to the present, in a sense seeking legitimacy for his music on the basis of its relation to the German masters of past centuries. In 1904, Karl Straube had edited a collection of seventeenth- and eighteenth-century organ music for C. F. Peters under the title *Alte Meister des Orgelspiels*, bearing the dedication "Dem jungen Meister Max Reger" prominently on the title page (see Figure 3.1). Reger thanked Straube in a letter of 11 September 1904, the rhetoric of which might easily have served to close the present essay: "You have given me such *enormous* pleasure in the endearing dedication of the Alte Meister! I have 1.) once again seen from this volume how great these old masters were, are, and *remain*, how in the face of this elemental Germanic strength (even in its graciousness) all of today's modern nonsense fizzles; 2.) as an egoist, I can put the collection to excellent use for my own purposes, in that I can still learn a *colossal* amount from it! I feel this dedication, therefore, to be not only a *very great* honor which you have bestowed upon me, … but also mainly as a *spur* to continue further upon my way; that is, to aim with all my might toward building *well* on the *only* proper foundation, that of the great *old* masters!" (Popp 1986: 66–67).

4. An Open Letter

1. It is useful to compare this sentiment to the disclaimer set at the end of essay 12 regarding the String Quartet in D minor op. 74, a work that "desires merely to be music."
2. "Schriftgelehrten" is Luther's term for the Jewish scribes of the New Testament whose rigid adherence to the law played a part in the conviction of Jesus. Note that this usage prepares for the imagery of "heretics and antichrists" later in the same paragraph. On Reger's use of religious allusion in his writing, see further the introduction.

3. The reference is to Shakespeare's *Love's Labour's Lost*, known to Reger in German as *Verlorene Liebesmüh*.
4. Matthew 5:3. Cf. "I Request the Floor!" note 8.
5. It is interesting to examine Reger's own "plain rule book" for modulation — the *Beiträge zur Modulationslehre* of 1903 (and the complementary essays 1 and 2) — in light of this comment, since it consists entirely of examples that are not supplemented by written-out rules. At various points earlier in the decade, Reger had cursorily entertained thoughts of producing a treatise on harmony, either independently or together with the Berlin theory instructor Wilhelm Klatte, but a real plan never developed; see further the introduction.
6. The line appears in chapter 15 ("Die Reue," or "Remorse") of Wilhelm Busch's popular illustrated story *Die fromme Helene (Busch 1872)*. Busch (1832–1908) authored the likewise popular *Max und Moritz (Busch 1865)*, the name of which was adopted by the piano duo of Reger and Phillip Wolfrum as a witty reference to their nonacademic Bach playing.
7. "Der deutsche Michel" emerged during the *Vormärz* as the symbol of German unity and of revolution guided by the will of the *Volk*. The sleeping Michel represented the opposite: a divided and oppressed people. By invoking the image of the waking Michel, Reger aligns the Wilhelminian era's optimistic notion of a progressive, united nation with a likewise forward-looking art, free from "mediocrity" and "reactionary backwardness."
8. Reger's disparaging remark is directed toward the Deutsche Arbeiterpartei (DAP), organized by Austria's German labor in Trautenau (Bohemia) in 1904 and already associated with national socialism long before its name was changed in 1918 to reflect that association (NSDAP, or Nationalsozialistische Deutsche Arbeiterpartei). Reger's political leanings have not been systematically explored as yet, but his word choice here suggests that his own nationalism, which shines through clearly in these essays, did not share the ideology of radical economic self-interest that defined the DAP in the Austrian lands. Cf. further "Hugo Wolf's Artistic Legacy," note 16.
9. The fictional German Kleinstadt of Krähwinkl (or Krähwinkel; in English approximately "Crow's Corner") had been, particularly since the revolutionary movements of the mid-nineteenth century, widely understood as the symbol of a naïve, comfortable German narrow-mindedness, and of the fundamental misunderstanding of the nature of freedom brought about by that narrow-mindedness. The Austrian

Johann Nestroy (1801–62) had adopted the name and subject matter from earlier playwrights like August von Kotzebue (*Die deutschen Kleinstädter*, 1802) and Adolf Bäuerle (*Die falsche Catalini in Krähwinkel*, 1818) for his popular farce *Freiheit in Krähwinkel* (1848). Here, Reger means to say that the "reactionary backwardness" that put Michel to sleep actually produces the illusion of progress and "freedom" in art, and hence the smug attitude of the critics, located of course in "Krähwinkl."

10. Reger alludes to the art periodical *Der Kunstwart: Rundschau über alle Gebiete des Schönen*, published 1887–94 by the Verlag Kunstwart in Dresden, and then from 1894 to 1937 by G. W. Callwey in Munich. Richard Batka and Georg Göhler, both ill disposed toward Reger's music, were active respectively as critic and editor for *Der Kunstwart* at the time. Hermann Wilske has called the paper "the intellectual center of the opposition to Reger" during his years in Munich (Wilske 1995: 163).
11. Published from 1848 through 1944, *Kladderadatsch* was a weekly satirical paper ideologically allied with Bismarck's political program. It took its name from a Berlin expression that referred to the falling over and shattering of an object. *Simplizissimus* (recte *Simplicissimus*, or "the greatest simpleton") was likewise a weekly paper with a satirical tone, published in Munich from 1896 through 1944. Regarding the latter, cf. the drafted ending of essay 7, "Hugo Wolf's Artistic Legacy," note 28."
12. Reger refers here to the period 1886–90, or from his entrance into the preparatory school at Weiden to the beginning of his studies with Hugo Riemann in Sondershausen. Whatever his sentiments toward the symphonic poem at the time, Reger's known compositional activity from the period falls decidedly on the side of so-called absolute music: the Ouvertüre in D minor ("Heroide") from 1889 may represent his most adventuresome foray into the aesthetic climes of Liszt and Strauss. For the most exact account of Reger's early development as documented by the original source materials, see Popp 2000: 21–60.
13. The expression is a form of Frederick the Great's often-cited ideal of enlightened political tolerance: "In meinem Staat soll ein jeder nach seiner Façon selig werden."
14. The wording modifies and reverses the motto "Frei aber froh" associated with Brahms, specifically with the musical cypher F-A(flat)-F that opens one of Reger's favorite Brahms works, the Third Symphony op. 90. It is not clear whether the association is intentional.
15. Reger's quarrels with the Munich chapter of the ADMV are representative of the rocky reception that met his music (and person) in that city during the century's first decade. He had been elected to the group early

in 1904 but had withdrawn his membership already by March 1906, citing intolerable political intrigues involving the ADMV's then vice president Max von Schillings.

16. Reger alludes to Hans Sachs's words in Act I of Wagner's *Die Meistersinger von Nürnberg*, where Sachs cites the time-honored regulation that "the marker will be so inclined that neither hatred nor love will cloud the judgment he renders [Der Merker werde so bestellt, / daß weder Haß noch Lieben / das Urteil trübe, das er fällt]." From 1910, Wagner's line would become the head motto of the Austrian periodical *Der Merker*.
17. See Reger's extended evaluation of Wolf and his development from three years earlier in essay 7, "Hugo Wolf's Artistic Legacy."
18. The reference is, of course, to the words of the Chorus mysticus at the end of *Faust* II, which read "The inadequate here is perfected [Das Unzulängliche,/hier wird's Ereignis]." Interestingly enough, Gustav Mahler had completed the Eighth Symphony, together with the choral setting of these words in its closing bars, precisely during the summer of 1907.
19. Reger was often strong in his criticism of what he perceived as an institutionalized unfriendliness toward his music. After his move to Leipzig, for instance, he would write in 1909 to one of the most influential members of the Leipzig Conservatory's board, Reinhold Anschütz, about the resistance of the conservatory to new music: "At the Royal School of Music in Berlin, which has the reputation of being so horribly backward, [Josef] Joachim at the time arranged for the performance of my *Serenade* op. 95 in the orchestra class. Recently they played there my *Hiller Variations* for orchestra op. 100 and Richard Strauss's *Tod und Verklärung*. One also plays zealously my piano pieces at other Berlin conservatories! Is anything like this happening here at our Royal Conservatory of Music? When??" (Letter of 30 October 1909 in Hase Koehler 1928: 218)
20. The reference has not come to light.
21. The turn of phrase was popular, in one form or another, as a way of underscoring the superiority of German intellectual life, stemming apparently from the German poet Wolfgang Menzel's study *Die deutsche Literatur* (Menzel 1836).

5. Hugo Riemann: Degeneration and Regeneration in Music

1. The expression, or some variant of it, served as a kind of mantra for the progressive optimism of the Kaiserreich around the turn of the century.

By introducing it here, Riemann announces his thesis in the clearest possible terms: namely, that a naïve notion of progress has masked a dangerous "degeneration" in art. The original expression is drawn from a well-known passage in Goethe's *Faust* I, where Wagner addresses Faust: "Pardon! it is a great pleasure / to place yourself in the spirit of the times, / to see how a wise man thought before us, / and how magnificently we after all have progressed [Verzeiht! es ist ein groß Ergetzen, / Sich in den Geist der Zeiten zu versetzen, / Zu schauen, wie vor uns ein weiser Mann gedacht, / Und wie wirs dann zuletzt so herrlich weit gebracht]."

2. The violinist and string quartet leader Ignaz Schuppanzigh (1776–1830) led the Augarten concerts from 1795.
3. Riemann had particularly pronounced opinions about the "mass training of the conservatories" and the negative implications of shortcuts to the necessary comprehensiveness of professional musicianship. In an earlier essay titled "Unsere Konservatorien," he had observed wryly, "If today on this end, one sticks in a farmer boy with even fingers and healthy ears, then after a year a polished composer or virtuoso must come out on the other" (Riemann 1895: 33).
4. "Kapellmeistermusik" was the term that distinguished, usually pejoratively, occasional music from so-called autonomous art. Riemann is arguing that the older aesthetic, based in comprehensive musicianship, has unfortuately given way to an increased specialization. It is worth noting that Riemann's pupil Reger would in fact "unite composer and conductor in a single person" with notable results during his years as leader of the Meininger Hofkapelle (1911–14).
5. In the sixth edition of his *Musik-Lexicon*, Riemann seems to have answered his own question with respect to Edvard Grieg (1843–1907) by remarking that he "is without question a composer of original, healthy talent and has written works full of poetry… ; it is therefore lamentable that he imposed upon himself the limitation of national characterization [die Beschränkung nationaler Charakteristik], rather than having created works of lasting general significance in the musical universal language!" (Riemann 1905: 497).
6. Riemann valued Max Bruch (1838–1920) particularly for his choral works.
7. According to Riemann, the works of Heinrich Hofmann (1842–1902) show "less original talent than a fine sense for beauty of sound" (ibid.: 577).

8. Of the major works by Friedrich Kiel (1821–85), Riemann writes, "Even if his major works do not show an outspoken artistic originality, but rather betray the composer's familiarity with Bach and Beethoven, often through a perhaps unconscious reliance, they nevertheless demonstrate such elevated mastery paired with strict criticism and his aesthetic instinct, that they undoubtedly lay claim to a place among the best of newer music" (ibid.: 653).
9. Joseph Rheinberger (1839–1901) composed works of "a thoroughly original character; a certain severity and austerity [Strenge und Herbheit] give them a breath of the classical" (ibid.: 1092).
10. According to Riemann, Heinrich von Herzogenberg (1843–1900) "no doubt strongly tended toward contrapuntal compositional techniques, but he still had enough of a sense for sound not to fall prey to the dangers arising from such a practice" (ibid.: 563).
11. Riemann wrote that the works of Joseph Joachim Raff (1822–82) had passed from favor more quickly that expected. "Already today and almost without exception, they have become obsolete. Compared to the works of the Classical and Romantic composers, also to those of Brahms, they have paled and disappear from programs. No doubt, his works are very uneven in quality, but it surely might be difficult to explain why, for example, even the Waldsymphonie [No. 3 "Im Walde" op. 153, 1869] no longer 'sounds' today" (ibid.: 1062).
12. Riemann's assessment of the pianist/composer Anton Rubinstein (1829–94) was: "His playing was imposing, enchanting, fascinating. As a composer, R. is a completely analogous figure. His intentions are always lofty, and his ideal lies less with beautiful sonorous effects than it does with gripping passion, less with formal perfection than with a powerful abundance of content. Sometimes even a certain preference for the baroque emerges.… Schumann must be the master to whom R. is most closely related, with the reservation that R. knows less how to strike the gentle strings than does the former" (ibid.: 1133).
13. Friedrich Robert Volkmann (1815–83), according to Riemann "one of the most distinguished recent composers," aligned himself with the relatively conservative styles of Schumann and Brahms (ibid.: 1416).

6. Degeneration and Regeneration in Music

1. The essay did not appear on 15 October as Reger suggests, but at the end of the same month.

2. The Genossenschaft deutscher Tonsetzer, or German Composers' Association, was founded on 14 January 1903 and was the first such German society to be concerned with composers' performance rights. The organization had sprung from an earlier society, the Genossenschaft deutscher Komponisten, formed in September 1898 by Richard Strauss, Hans Sommer (1837–1922), and Friedrich Rösch (1862–1925), among others.
3. During his period of study under Riemann, Reger became intimately acquainted with his mentor's idiosyncratic theories of phrasing and meter, as well as with his editorial policies. See, e.g., Figure 6.1, and his letter of 11 April 1890 to his former teacher Adalbert Lindner in Popp 2000: 62–65. Whereas Reger himself adopted certain aspects of Riemann's complex system into his notation early on (see, e.g., the early organ chorale preludes on "O Traurigkeit, O Herzeleid" and "Komm, süßer Tod" from 1893/94), he dropped them soon after. From Reger's perspective, his own *Urtext* scores were notationally unproblematical, especially compared to Riemann's editions of the masterworks. However, on Reger's characteristic wish to clarify his notation with the aid of words, see the introduction.
4. Although an outspoken critic of Bruckner, Eduard Hanslick (1825–1904) appears to have advanced such a comment not about Bruckner's music, but rather about Tchaikovsky's Violin Concerto in D major op. 35, in Vienna's *Neue Freie Presse* of 5 December 1881: "Friedrich Vischer once observed, speaking of obscene pictures, that they stink to the eye. Tchaikovsky's Violin Concerto gives us for the first time the hideous notion that there can be music that stinks to the ear" (cited in Slonimsky 1953: 207). The translation is Slonimsky's.
5. Reger's categorical statement does not account for the nuances of his former mentor's actual views of Liszt, with whom Riemann had corresponded in the 1870s. In the 1905 edition of his *Musik-Lexicon*, Riemann had written, "Although L.'s compositions are much less the product of a spontaneous creative urge than of sophisticated reflection, his high culture and enormous knowledge of literature as well as his warm enthusiasm for progressive ideals (the negation of all rule systems, striving for characterization) have nevertheless pressed upon them the stamp of originality. Admittedly, in his piano compositions he often loses himself in empty sound play" (Riemann 1905: 780).
6. I agree with Susanne Shigihara, who in her edition of the present essay points out that this image — emerging in Riemann and developed further by Reger — appears to anticipate Wassily Kandinsky's movement

"Der Blaue Reiter," formed in 1911 (Shigihara 1990: 258). Kandinsky had painted *Le chevalier bleu* already in 1903, with its phantom blue-clad horseman riding a white horse to the left. The movement would have important points of contact with Arnold Schoenberg's music, but clearly the notion of "riding left" was alive in Reger's circle as well. Cf. Reger's reference to "mounting Pegasus" in essay 4, "An Open Letter," and H. Starkloff's caricature from 1913, *Max Reger auf dem Pegasus, die Schranken der Konvention überspringend*, reproduced in (among several sources) Shigihara 1990: 240.

7. Obviously forging an ideological link with the Leipzig Collegium musicum of J. S. Bach, Riemann gave the same name to his musicological research institute at the University of Leipzig, leading the way for the foundation of other such "Collegia" in academic institutions as the twentieth century progressed and interest in early music spread. Riemann's Collegium aimed at the revival of Baroque music by means of both performance and publication. As a student, Reger had been involved in the "historische Konzerte" Riemann produced at the Wiesbaden Conservatory during the first half of the 1890s, and he was not enthusiastic about the aims of historical performance.
8. In 1900, Reger had dedicated his organ *Fantasy and Fugue on BACH* op. 46 to Rheinberger, and he had served as the elder composer's successor at the Munich Akademie in 1905–6, teaching composition, counterpoint, and organ. On Rheinberger's problematical reception, see Wolfgang Horn's "Die Rolle Josef Rheinbergers in Musikgeschichten zum 19. Jahrhundert" (Horn 2004). On the development of Rheinberger's image in Reger's circles during this period, see Christopher Anderson's "Ehre und Unterordnung: Josef Rheinberger unter den Organisten der Leipziger Straube-Schule" (Anderson 2004a).
9. Nowhere does Reger more forcefully advance an image of himself as "radical progressive" than in this essay, answering the views of academia, the bastion of creative backwardness itself. It is important to bear in mind that Reger would significantly alter this posture by the end of the decade, in the face of Schoenberg's departure from tonality in the *Drei Klavierstücke* op. 11, with unavoidable ramifications for his musical style, particularly from the time of the Violin Sonata in C minor op. 139 onward. Quite literally on the last day of the decade, he wrote to the pianist August Stradal of Schoenberg's op. 11, "I know the three piano pieces…; I myself can no longer go along with this. Whether this kind of thing can still be granted the name of music, I do not know: my mind is really too old fashioned for it! Now emerges all the misunderstood

Strauss and other such affairs! Oh, it's time to become conservative [O, es ist zum Konservativwerden]" (letter of 31 December 1910 in Hase-Koehler 1928: 238). "Wobbly bones" or not, Reger and his horse had by that time in fact yielded, at least ideologically, somewhat to the right.

10. Because of Riemann's prominent position, Reger's sharp critique of his views did not fail to incite reaction in the press. Among the pieces appearing in the wake of the "Degeneration" exchange was a brief answer by Riemann himself, published in the *Neue Musik-Zeitung* of 21 November 1907, in which the latter asked "How does Herr Reger come to identify himself with the 'rider to the left?' Has it not occured to him that in fact there is a rider in the middle, of whose wobbly bones the legend knows nothing? However, with Reger's declaration to the banner of Richard Strauss, which comes as a complete surprise to me, the intent of my little article has entirely liquefied [gründlich zu Wasser geworden]" (Riemann 1907b, cited in Shigihara 1990: 299). A more extended article by the Riemann pupil Karl Mennicke appeared under the cynical title "Max Reger als Retter in der Not!" in the *Neue Zeitschrift für Musik* of 2 January 1908, in which Mennicke asserted, "One fears, unfortunately, that this man, who has become great overnight, regresses inwardly.... There was no cause — and there will never be one — to disgrace Germany's leading historian and theoretician with a tasteless pasquinade in order to set his own splendor in greater relief" (cited in ibid.: 335). Finally and most dramatically, in 1910 the Leipzig critic Walter Niemann published an exceedingly negative article about Reger (Niemann 1910), against which the composer pursued legal action, resulting in Niemann's apology and admission that the tone of his essay stemmed from Reger's harsh answer to Riemann.

7. Hugo Wolf's Artistic Legacy

1. In 1895 Wolf composed the four-act opera *Der Corregidor* on a libretto by Rosa Mayreder after Alarcón's *El sombrero de tres picos*. The work was staged by the Munich Hofoper under Hugo Röhr in November 1903.
2. Reger here refers to the 1904 monument by Edmund von Hellmer erected at Wolf's grave in Vienna's Zentralfriedhof.
3. The reference is to the Epistle of James 5:2: "Your riches are corrupted and your garments are moth-eaten [Euer Reichtum ist verfault, eure Kleider sind von Motten zerfressen]" and to the Gospel of Matthew 6:19: "Lay not up for yourselves treasures upon earth, where moth and rust doth corrupt, and where thieves break through and steal [Ihr sollt

euch nicht Schätze sammeln auf Erden, wo sie die Motten und der Rost fressen und wo die Diebe einbrechen und stehlen]."

4. The source of the citation has not come to light. In the original, Reger added, "after they had been assaulted outright after the first hearing [nachdem man dieselben beim ersten Hören in Grund und Boden verwettert hatte]."
5. Reger here possibly refers to the Danish composer and conductor Eduard Lassen (1830–1904), who had followed Franz Liszt in the post of music director in Weimar. Lassen died on 15 January, about a month before the publication of this essay. Later in the autograph text, Reger made a disparaging remark about Lassen's compositions, which was edited out in the published version. See further note 8.
6. Reger's association of Pfitzner with the ideal of the misunderstood genius, an association usually reserved for himself or for historical figures, was undoubtedly motivated by the friendship of the *Süddeutsche Monatshefte*'s editor Paul Nikolaus Cossmann with Pfitzner, who also worked on the editorial board of the new periodical. Even though Pfitzner's name would reappear among the "progressives" in essay 6 (the reply to Hugo Riemann of 1907), Reger's opinion of his music would soon sour (Müller 1993: 365, note 2).
7. The sentence originally read "Even cases like that of last winter's affair — of course arising in Berlin — involving Prof. Dr. H. Reimann, or the critic's opinion (!?!) of a few weeks ago in one of the most circulated Berlin papers that Beethoven's op. 106 is *'an ungrateful étude'* — even these cases are not able to shake the German newspaper reader's beliefs, which alone confer salvation [Selbst Fälle wie die vorigen Winter natürlich in Berlin zu verzeichnende Affaire des Prof. Dr. H. Reimann oder die vor einigen Wochen in einem der gelesensten Berliner Blätter seitens des Herrn Musikreferenten verbrechene Ansicht (!?!), daß Beethoven's Op. 106 *'ein undankbarer Studienwerk'* sei, — vermögen den alleinseligmachenden Glauben des deutschen leider nur viel zu oft urteilslosen Zeitungslesers nicht zu erschüttern]." Heinrich Reimann (1850–1906) had been active in Berlin since 1887 as a music scholar, critic, and organist. In 1893, Reimann had published a favorable if cautious review of Reger's opp. 1–4 and 6, and he had been the major organ teacher of Karl Straube (1873–1950), arguably Reger's strongest advocate early in his career. Neither the nature of the "affair" nor the name of the critic addressing Beethoven's op. 106 is known.
8. The original sentence read "… from those justifiably so beloved, singable, and pleasing songs of Hildach, Lassen, etc., etc. — and that these

songs of this 'diminished 6/4 chord fad-monger' could never interest a wider audience — [… als die mit Recht so beliebten sanglichen, gefälligen Lieder von Hildach Lassen etc. etc. — , daß diese Gesänge dieser 'verminderten Quartsextaccordfexen' niemals weitere Kreise zu interessieren vermöchten —]." The German baritone Eugen Hildach (1849–1924) was prominent at the time as a singer and composer of salon songs. Erik Meyer-Hellmund (1861–1932) was a Russian singer and prolific composer in several genres; his works include over two hundred songs, here characterized by Reger as "sanglich" and "gefällig," i.e., lacking substance. On Eduard Lassen, see note 5. It seems reasonable that the omission of the latter's name in the published version stems from his death in January.

9. Here Reger had included a parenthetical remark, "that a general shaking of the head would have emerged and even the critic admits that he would have to leave the matter with the honest Kothner's statement ('Yes, I understood nothing of it!') — [daß sich allgemeines Schütteln des Kopfes erhoben hätte u. auch der Referent bekennt, daß es mit dem Ausspruch des biederen Kothner ('Ja, ich verstand gar nichts daran!') bewenden lassen müßte —]." Not insignificantly, Reger had lifted this statement almost word-for-word from a review of Edgar Istel, published in the *Neue Zeitschrift für Musik* on 18 November 1903 (Istel 1903: 609). There, Istel's words do not refer to Wolf at all (although the review does address the Munich premiere of Wolf's *Der Corregidor*), but rather to the premiere of Reger's own Violin Sonata in C major op. 72. See further the introduction. The reference is of course to Wagner's character Fritz Kothner in *Die Meistersinger von Nürnberg*, who in Act I admits ignorance to the construction of Walther's love song. Reger misquotes slightly: Kothner's line (accurately reproduced by Istel) reads "Ja, ich verstand gar nichts davon."
10. Überbrettl was a Berlin-based caberet that formed part of the "Buntes Theater" of Ernst von Wolzogen, author of Richard Strauss's *Feuersnot* libretto and half brother to Hans Freiherr von Wolzogen, a prolific writer on Wagner's music. Writers such as Richard Dehmel and Frank Wedekind were associated with Überbrettl, and Arnold Schoenberg had taken a position with the caberet after December 1901. Reger, however, associates it with musical degeneracy based on a market-driven music industry foreign to art.
11. The autograph text continues at this point "… such as are still today occasionally heard in the 'home territory of the softening of the brain' [… wie sie gelegentlich noch heute in den 'Heimstätten der Gehirnerwei-

chung' zu hören sind]." Reger's low opinion of Berlin's musical culture rests in large part with his profound distaste for the Jewish element that controlled its presses.

12. The figure is somewhat exaggerated: Henri Hinrichsen of C. F. Peters had purchased the rights to the *Mörike-Lieder*, the *Italienisches Liederbuch*, the *Goethe-Lieder*, and the *Michelangelo-Lieder* for 153,975 marks (Lawford-Hinrichsen 2000: 112–13).
13. The latter two sentences appeared originally, in a rather more drawn out version, after the poem of Gustav Falke cited toward the end of the essay. There, Reger had identified the "yearly interest" as 8,000 marks.
14. Wolf completed his *Christnacht* (cantata for soloists, mixed chorus, and orchestra) in 1889 on a text by August Graf von Platen-Hallermünde. A revised version of the work had appeared in 1903 with Lauterbach and Kuhn in Leipzig, edited by Reger and F. Foll. Reger himself would lead a performance of the work — presumably in his own edition — at the Munich Odeon on 15 December 1905 with the Porges-Gesangverein and the Kaim-Orchester. Aside from an early concert on 19 November 1898 at which Reger conducted his own *Hymne an den Gesang* op. 21 in his hometown of Weiden, the Munich concert, which included works of Liszt alongside Wolf's *Christnacht*, constitutes Reger's debut as a conductor (O. and I. Schreiber 1981a: 292). The relevant reviews are reproduced in O. and I. Schreiber 1981b: 105–7.
15. Wolf's choruses are from 1881, and Reger had produced a version of them for male chorus in 1903, published by Lauterbach and Kuhn.
16. Johann Wenzel Kalliwoda (1801–66) was a Bohemian violinist and composer who worked for much of his life in Germany. His works include seven symphonies and two operas, and some of his music found favor with Robert Schumann, who dedicated his Intermezzos op. 4 to Kalliwoda. The *Deutsches Lied* for male chorus became a symbol of German nationalism in Bohemia and maintained its popularity during Reger's time. On this and the following sentence, cf. Reger's sentiments concerning nationalism and the Deutsche Arbeiterpartei in "An Open Letter," note 8.
17. This sentence does not appear in the autograph text, and the choral society is unidentified.
18. Wolf composed the D-minor Quartet between 1878 and 1884. Reger could have pointed out that the first movement bears a motto that supports the image of the suffering artist he draws: Goethe's words "Entbehren sollst du, sollst entbehren" are associated with Faust's renunciation of all human love in his pact with Satan (*Faust* I).

19. Besides the *Christnacht* oratorio and the Eichendorff choruses, Lauterbach and Kuhn had acquired the rights to Wolf's String Quartet in D minor, the *Italienische Serenade*, and *Penthesilea*. Reger set to work on arrangements and editions of all these works, and the present essay functions in part to increase awareness and market for precisely those works of Wolf edited by Reger that would appear with Lauterbach. Reger's comment at this point in his original text — "(ebenfalls bei Lauterbach und Kuhn erschienen)" — was edited out in the published version, as were similar references to Lauterbach in connection with the works discussed subsequently, possibly to avoid the impression that the essay served more nearly as a kind of advertisement for Lauterbach's catalog than it did as a retrospective on Wolf's work per se. In any case, Reger had commented to his publishers in October of the previous year that "my article on Hugo Wolf's legacy could be *very* useful to you" (postcard of 17 October 1903 in Müller 1993: 228)!
20. In 1903, thirteen of Wolf's unpublished songs appeared with Lauterbach and Kuhn under the title *Lieder aus der Jugendzeit*, edited by F. Foll.
21. The autograph's prolix version of this sentence gives a better flavor of the original rather untamed style: "Die Jugendlieder Wolfs geben den jüngsten 'Titanen' (?!?), welche junge Herren ja symphonische Dichtungen, Symphonien, große Gesänge nur mit Orchester in einem Alter gebären, in dem andere gewöhnliche Sterbliche, denen das ungestüme Ausdrucksbedürfnis, das nur mit größtem Orchester da befriedigt werden kann erst viel später zum Bewustsein kommt, noch die harten Schulbänke 'zieren,' die fatale Lehre 'Klein beginnen, groß endigen.'"
22. Wolf planned his *Italienische Serenade* as a four-movement work for string quartet, with the first movement completed in 1887. The version of the piece for small orchestra is in fact the "arrangement," dating from 1892. Originally, Reger had added a phrase at the end of the sentence: "... and a marvelous four-hand arrangment for piano (by Karl Straube) will delight all friends of genial domestic music [... und eine famose Bearbeitung für Klavier zu vier Händen (von Karl Straube) wird sich das Entzücken aller Freunde geistvoller Hausmusik erregen]." Reger, rather than his close friend Karl Straube, at the time organist of St. Thomas Church in Leipzig, prepared the arrangement. There appears to be no evidence that Reger ever played or led a performance of Wolf's work.
23. *Penthesilea* was composed between 1883 and 1885 on the model of Liszt's symphonic poems. The first published version of the piece, and the one to which Reger refers subsequently, was that edited by Joseph

Hellmesberger for Lauterbach in 1903, containing heavy revisions and substantial cuts to the unique formal structure of the original. From the Hellmesberger edition, Reger published a four-hand piano arrangement of the work with Lauterbach in the same year. Wolf's original score appeared first in 1936, edited by Robert Haas for the Musikwissenschaftlicher Verlag of Leipzig. Reger appears never to have performed the work in any form.

24. *Penthesilea* had appeared first in Munich only the previous month, on 20 January under Felix Weingartner.
25. Wolf planned to compose Moritz Hoernes's libretto based on Alarcón's *El niño de la bola* as the three-act opera *Manuel Venegas*. Five scenes from Act I were completed in 1897, but the project did not advance further.
26. The original clause began "If finally I give the happiest and most sincere recognition to all those who have earned such great merit in the service of Hugo Wolf's art — and this at a time when one nearly runs the danger of a mental evaluation for such support — then I hope to act in the spirit of all those, who… [Wenn ich schließlich allen deren, die sich um die Kunst Hugo Wolfs solch große Verdienste erworben haben u. das noch zu einer Zeit, in der man beinahe in Gefahr gerät, deshalb auf den Geisteszustand untersucht zu werden, da freudigst u. aufrichtigste Anerkennung erspreche, so hoffe ich damit im Sinne aller derjenigen zu handeln, die …]."
27. In the autograph text, Reger includes only a reference to where the poem may be found — "(Tanz und Andacht, pag 142, 143)" — in the 1893 edition of Falke's work published by Albert of Munich, where the piece appears as the 89th poem of a set of "Vermischte Gedichte." For the complete poem see Falke 1893: 142–43. Gustav Falke (1853–1916) was a poet and piano teacher whose texts were set by a number of composers. Reger drew upon his poetry between 1894 and 1909 for songs and choruses in the collections of opp. 15, 39, 43, 55, 62, 68, 70, 75, and 76/4.
28. The final paragraph differed greatly in the original version:

    We hope that the German people (and before them the German musician) will now strive untiringly to repay the spirit of the unfortunate composer in overabundance for all the disconsolate, bitter wounds, all the unspeakable wrongs strewn over the thorny life's path of Hugo Wolf; that our German musicians will bury all strife and enmity, all envy and jealousy, in order to unite behind the duty: "To honor, to admire the great master, the true high priest of art, Hugo Wolf!"

* Those with a healthy sense of humor are informed of one further fact. After the performance of Bach's double concerto for two violins on 30 November 1903 in the Kaimsaal [undoubtedly BWV 1043 in D minor with the Munich Kaim Orchestra under Felix Weingartner], certain 'music experts' hissed! Should this hissing have been meant for J. S. Bach, we ask the editors of *Simplizissimus* to acquire portraits of these persons for the "Gallery of Famous Contemporaries."

******

I ask unconditionally that the paragraph marked * be included as a note!

[Hoffen wir, daß das deutsche Volk (vorab der deutsche Musiker) nun mit unermüdlichen Eifer bestrebt sein wird, all die trostlosen, bitteren Wunden, all das unsägliche Unrecht, womit Hugo Wolfs dornenvoller Lebensweg so erbarmlich bekrängt war, endlich an den Manen des unglücklichen Tondichters in überreichene Maße wieder gut zu machen, daß unsere deutschen Musiker allen Hader u. Zwist, allen Neid u. jede Mißgunst begraben, um einig zu werden in der Verpflichtung: 'Zu ehren, zu bewundern den großen Meister, den wahrhaften Hohenpriester der Kunst: Hugo Wolf!'

* Freunden gesunden Humors sei noch folgende Thatsache mitgetheilt: Am 30. Nov. 1903 wurde im Kaimsaale nach dem Vortrag des Bachschen Doppelkonzerts für 2 Violinen von einigen "Musikkennern" gezischt! Sollte dieses "Zischen" J. S. Bach gegolten haben, so bitten wir die Redaktion des "Simplizissimus," sich die Portraits dieser Persönlichkeiten für die "Gallerie berühmter Zeitgenossen" zu verschaffen.

******

Ich bitte den Absatz * als Anmerkung unten unbedingt hin zu setzen!]

On the satirical Munich newspaper *Simplicissimus*, see essay 4, "An Open Letter," note 11.

29. Though they do not appear in the manuscript text, these lines from Hölderlin's poem "Menschenbeifall" serve to close the published version. I have used the translation of Emily Ezust, set by Benjamin Britten in the *Six Hölderlin Fragments* op. 61.

8. On April 1

1. For the location of, and access to, this article I am indebted to Dr. Stephan Hörner of the Gesellschaft für bayerische Musikgeschichte in Munich.
2. On a visit to Athens in the autumn of 1903, Duncan had recruited a troupe of Greek boys to reproduce the choruses of ancient drama. In her autobiography, she recounts that the northern regions did not agree with the boys' constitutions, and that they eventually began:

> feeling the effects of their unaccustomed environment.... It seems that they asked continually for black bread, black ripe olives and raw onions, and when these condiments were not in their daily menu, they became enraged with the waiters — going so far as to throw beefsteaks at their heads and attack them with knives.... [O]ne day, after much worried consultation, we came to the decision to march all our Greek Chorus down to Wertheimer's big Department Store. We bought them all nice ready-made knickerbockers for the short boys and long trousers for the big boys, and then took them in taxis to the railroad station and, putting them all in second-class carriages, with a ticket for each to Athens, bade them a fond farewell. After their departure we put off the revival of Ancient Greek Music to a later date .... (Duncan 1927: 138–40)

3. Reger had written the same comment to his publishers Lauterbach and Kuhn in a letter of the same day (letter of 1 April 1904 in Müller 1993: 305), and he felt compelled to follow up on the reaction against his essay later that year (letter of 6 November 1904 in ibid.: 401).
4. The eastern Riviera, on the Genoese eastern coast.
5. Aringsdorf is presumably a fictional village, but the Austrian town of Kufstein is located in the Tirol, northeast of Innsbruck on the Bavarian border.
6. In February 1896 ("8 years ago"), Reger had made the personal acquaintance of both Ferruccio Busoni and Richard Strauss, and in April of that year, he had corresponded with Johannes Brahms, an exchange that meant a great deal to the young composer.
7. The date of 21 October 1903 is undoubtedly significant with respect to Duncan, especially since Reger mentions it twice in close proximity. Perhaps this is the date of one of Duncan's first appearances in Munich.
8. Reger means the account of Saul's conversion to Christianity in The Acts of the Apostles 9, according to which Saul was blinded by a

heavenly light on the road to Damascus and regained sight at the hand of Ananias three days later, now able to "see" the truth.

9. Among them, of course, Johannes Brahms, whom Reger had "met" by correspondence eight years previously, in 1896.
10. The Soxhlet extractor was invented in 1879 by the German chemist Franz Ritter von Soxhlet (1848–1926) and is used to extract certain compounds (typically lipid) from solids. Soxhlet also happens to have proposed the application of Louis Pasteur's "pasteurization" process to milk in 1886.
11. This is one of a handful of works from the *Well-Tempered Clavier* that Reger seems to have played more or less regularly in public.

9. Felix Mendelssohn Bartholdy's *Songs without Words*

1. Cf. essay 4, "An Open Letter," note 3.
2. The Six Sonatas op. 65 appeared simultaneously in Germany, France, Italy, and England in 1845, and they certainly constituted a part of Reger's early musical education. During his student days under Hugo Riemann, Reger had issued a qualified judgment of Mendelssohn's organ music to George Augener: "In my opinion (which Herr Dr. Riemann also shares) we have in no way made progress in organ style since J. S. Bach. We have regressed in this respect — for example, Mendelssohn has passages here and there in his organ things that are not entirely in keeping with the organ — this way of writing was continued by Rheinberger…" (letter of 8 December 1892 in Popp 2000: 129). Still, Reger would recall to Theodor Kroyer in 1902 that he had played "the complete organ works of Bach and Mendelssohn" (letter of 26 December 1902, cited in Wilske 1995: 85) by the early 1880s, a claim that is certainly impossible to take literally but that must say something important about the position of Mendelssohn as an organ composer in Reger's mind.
3. Reger owned a volume (C. F. Peters 1761), preserved at the Max-Reger-Archiv (Sammlung Musikgeschichte) of the Meininger Museen-Schloß Elisabethenburg, containing the overtures *Ein Sommernachtstraum* op. 21, *Die Fingals-Höhle (Hebriden)* op. 26, *Meeresstille und glückliche Fahrt* op. 27, *Die schöne Melusine* op. 32, and *Ruy Blas* op. 95 in the edition of F. A. Roitzsch. Of these the opp. 21 and 26 — also the two mentioned by Reger in the present essay — bear extensive entries in his hand, including mild instances of reorchestration. During Reger's years as Hofkapellmeister at

Meiningen (late 1911 through early 1914), op. 21 appeared on concerts of the Hofkapelle nine times, op. 26 a single time.

4. Cf. Reger's comments along these lines regarding Edvard Grieg, Max Bruch, Heinrich Hofmann, Friedrich Kiel, and Joseph Rheinberger in essay 6, "Degeneration and Regeneration in Music," and his comment to Augener in a letter from 1892 in note 2 above.
5. There is no evidence that this is so, at least not "very often" or with respect to public performance. Exceptionally, on 8 February 1909 — about a week after the publication of this essay — Reger did program three *Lieder ohne Worte* on a chamber music concert given with Edgar Wollgandt and Julius Klengel in Jena (O. and I. Schreiber 1981a: 336).
6. A view Reger shared with Hugo Riemann: see Riemann's comments in essay 5.
7. It is worth noting that Reger's own piano touch was consistently cited, by supporters and detractors alike, as extraordinarily delicate. For a summary of contemporary commentary, see Wilske 1995: 45–70.
8. Hans von Bülow (1830–94) had edited some of Mendelssohn's works for piano, including the *Capriccio* in F-sharp minor op. 5 and the *Rondo capriccioso* op. 14. See also Theodor Pfeiffer's interesting account of Bülow's teaching of Mendelssohn (Pfeiffer 1894).
9. "Ehret eure deutschen Meister" derives, of course, from Hans Sachs's final admonition to Walther in Act III of Wagner's *Die Meistersinger von Nürnberg.*

12. String Quartet Op. 74 in D Minor

1. Compare Reger's comment at the outset of his later appreciation of Mendelssohn (essay 9), according to which "technical" analyses "almost always betray infinite acumen but usually amount to wasted effort."
2. The line is misquoted with respect to rhythm. The e^2 of bar 35 is actually a dotted quarter tied to a quarter.
3. Reger produces the theme here an octave lower than composed.
4. The quarter notes are harmonized as double stops.
5. Played in octaves beginning on d^1 and d, respectively.
6. Herta Müller has pointed out the connection of this frequently cited statement — a mantra for the cause of "absolute" music — to a comment Reger made to Carl Lauterbach and Max Kuhn just before the Frankfurt festival: "*Please*, read what I have written concerning my op. 74 in *Die Musik* no. 16 pages 244–247! I have a feeling that we will experience

in Frankfurt a 'mass burial' of the symphonic poem as such!" (Postcard of 20 May 1904 in Müller 1993: 319)

13. *Variations and Fugue on a Theme of Joh. Seb. Bach* for piano, two hands op. 81; and *Variations and Fugue on a Theme of Beethoven* for two pianos, four hands op. 86

1. Reger drew the theme for op. 81 from the duet for contralto and tenor (with oboe d'amore obbligato) "Seine Allmacht zu ergründen, wird sich kein Mensche finden," from Cantata BWV 128, *Auf Christi Himmelfahrt allein*. The theme of op. 86 issues from Beethoven's Bagatelle op. 119 no. 11.
2. Whereas the ADMV's program books typically reproduce themes or thematic complexes with little or no commentary, the witty sarcasm is unmistakably "Regerian."

Bibliography

Abraham, G. 1938; 2nd ed. 1949. *A Hundred Years of Music.* London: Duckworth.

Anderson, C. 2004a. "Ehre und Unterordnung: Josef Rheinberger unter den Organisten der Leipziger Straube-Schule." In *Josef Rheinberger: Werk und Wirkung*, ed. S. Hörner and H. Schick, 373-395. Tutzing: Hans Schneider.

——— 2004b. "'...wie ein Anatom mit dem Seziermesser...': Betrachtungen zur 'Meininger' Klangästhetik Max Regers." In *Reger-Studien 7: Festschrift für Susanne Popp*, ed. S. Schmalzriedt and J. Schaarwächter, 457–475. Stuttgart: Carus.

Arend, M. 1903–4a. Review of Max Reger, *Beiträge zur Modulationslehre. Blätter für Haus- und Kirchenmusik* 8/5: 78–79.

——— 1903–4b. Review of Max Reger, *Beiträge zur Modulationslehre. Blätter für Haus- und Kirchenmusik* 8/7: 112.

——— 1937. "Max Reger in Wiesbaden 1892/1893." *Mitteilungen der Max-Reger-Gesellschaft* 14: 4–8.

Busch, W. 1872. *Die fromme Melene.* Heidelberg: F. Bassermann.

——— 1865. *Max und Moritz: eine Bubengeschichte in sieben Streichen.* Munich: Braun und Schneider.

Cadenbach, R. 1991. *Max Reger und seine Zeit.* Laaber: Laaber-Verlag.

Dahlhaus, C. 1979. *Zwischen Romantik und Moderne: Vier Studien zur Musikgeschichte des späteren 19. Jahrhunderts.* M. Whittall, trans. 1980. *Between Romanticism and Modernism.* Berkeley: University of California Press.

——— 1973. "Warum ist Regers Musik so schwer verständlich?" *Neue Zeitschrift für Musik* 134/3: 134.

Duncan, I. 1927. *My Life*. New York: Liveright.

Falke, G. 1893. *Tanz und Andacht: Gedichte aus Tag und Traum*. Munich: E. Albert.

Gurlitt, W. and Hudemann, H.-O., eds. 1952. *Karl Straube: Briefe eines Thomaskantors*. Stuttgart: Koehler.

Hase-Koehler, E. von, ed. 1928. *Max Reger: Briefe eines deutschen Meisters*. Leipzig: Koehler und Amelang.

Haselböck, L. 2000. *Analytische Untersuchungen zur motivischen Logik bei Max Reger*. Wiesbaden: Breitkopf.

Hasse, K. 1921. *Max Reger: Mit acht eigenen Aufsätzen von Max Reger, sowie zehn Vollbildern in Autotypie und drei Handschriften-Nachbildungen*. Leipzig: Siegel.

Helm, J. 1870. *Allgemeine Musik- und Harmonielehre*. Nuremberg: Löhe.

Horn, W. 2004. "Die Rolle Josef Rheinbergers in Musikgeschichten zum 19. Jahrhundert." In *Josef Rheinberger: Werk und Wirkung*, ed. S. Hörner and H. Schick, 9-31. Tutzing: Hans Schneider.

Istel, E. 1903. Review of Max Reger, Violin Sonata in C major op. 72. *Neue Zeitschrift für Musik* 70/47: 608.

Lawford-Hinrichsen, I. 2000. *Music Publishing and Patronage: C. F. Peters: 1800 to the Holocaust*. Kenton, UK: Edition Press.

Mendelssohn Bartholdy, E. 1956. "Erinnerungen an Max Reger." *Mitteilungen des Max-Reger-Instituts* 4: 6–9.

Mueller von Asow, H., and E. H., eds. 1949. *Max Reger: Briefwechsel mit Herzog Georg II. von Sachsen-Meiningen*. Weimar: Hermann Böhlaus Nachfolger.

Müller, H., ed.. 1993. *Max Reger: Briefe an die Verleger Lauterbach & Kuhn*, vol. 1. Bonn: Dümmler.

Niemann, W. 1910. "Max Reger." *Der Türmer* 12/18: 273–78.

Pfeiffer, T. 1894. *Studien bei Hans von Bülow*. Berlin: Luckhardt. Richard Zimdars, trans. 1993. *The Piano Master Classes of Hans von Bülow: Two Participants' Accounts*. Bloomington: Indiana University Press.

Popp, S., ed.. 2000. *Der junge Reger: Briefe und Dokumente vor 1900*. Wiesbaden: Breitkopf und Härtel.

——— ed.. 1986. *Max Reger: Briefe an Karl Straube*. Bonn: Dümmler.

——— ed.. 1982. *Max Reger: Briefe an Fritz Stein*. Bonn: Dümmler.

Popp, S., and Shigihara, S., eds. 1995. *Max Reger: Briefwechsel mit dem Verlag C. F. Peters*. Bonn: Dümmler.

Quidde, M. 1904. "Miss Isadora Duncan und Beethoven." *Münchner Zeitung* 59 (11 March 1904): 5.

Reger, M. 1914. Response to "Festheft zum 50. Geburtstag von Richard Strauss." *Der Merker* 5/112: 394.

——— 1913. "Römischer Triumphgesang für Männerchor und Orchester, op. 126." *Die Musik* 12/17: 301.

——— 1912. Response to "Unsere Strauß-Rundfrage 'Worin liegt nach Ihrer Meinung die eigentliche Bedeutung von Richard Strauß' bisherigem Schaffen für die musikalische Fortentwickelung nach Wagner und Liszt?'" *Allgemeine Musik-Zeitung* 39/43: 1070.

——— 1910a. "Der 100. Psalm für Chor, Orchester und Orgel, op. 106." *Die Musik* 9/16: 225.

——— 1910b. "Quartett für Violine, Bratsche, Violoncello und Pianoforte, op. 113." *Die Musik* 9/16: 248–49.

——— 1909. "Felix Mendelssohn Bartholdys 'Lieder ohne Worte.'" *Illustrierte Zeitung Leipzig* 3422: 152–53.

——— 1907a. "Degeneration und Regeneration in der Musik." *Neue Illustrierte Musik-Zeitung* 29/3: 49–51.

——— 1907b. "Musik und Fortschritt." *Leipziger Tageblatt* (16 June 1907).

——— 1907c. "Offener Brief." *Die Musik* 7/1: 10–14.

——— 1905a. Response to "Bach-Umfrage 'Was ist mir Johann Sebastian Bach und was bedeutet er für unsere Zeit'" *Die Musik* 5/1: 74.

——— 1905b. "Variationen und Fuge über ein Thema von Joh. Seb. Bach für Klavier zu zwei Händen op. 81," and "Variationen und Fuge über ein Thema von Beethoven für zwei Pianoforte zu vier Händen op. 86." *Die Musik* 4/17: 316–17.

——— 1904a. "Hugo Wolfs künstlerischer Nachlass." *Süddeutsche Monatshefte* 1/2: 157–64; reprinted with autograph facsimile in O. Schreiber, ed. 1966. *Mitteilungen des Max-Reger-Instituts* 15: 2–44.

——— 1904b. "Ich bitte ums Wort!" *Neue Zeitschrift für Musik* 71/2: 20–21.

——— 1904c. "Mehr Licht." *Neue Zeitschrift für Musik* 71/11: 202–3.

——— 1904d. "Streichquartett op. 74 in d-moll." *Die Musik* 3/16: 244–47.

——— 1904e. *Supplement to the Theory of Modulation*. Trans. J. Bernhoff. Leipzig: C. F. Kahnt Nachfolger.

——— 1904f. "Zum 1. April." *Neue Zeitschrift für Musik* 71/14: 274–75.

——— 1903; 2nd ed. 1904. *Beiträge zur Modulationslehre*. Leipzig: C. F. Kahnt Nachfolger.

Richter, E. F. 1853. *Lehrbuch der Harmonie: Praktische Anleitung zu den Studien in derselben*. Leipzig: Breitkopf.

Riemann, H. 1907a. "Degeneration und Regeneration in der Musik." *Max Hesses Deutscher Musikerkalendar 1908*, 136–38.

——— 1907b. Response to "Degeneration und Regeneration in der Musik." *Neue Musik-Zeitung* 29/4: 87.

——— 1905. *Musik-Lexicon: 6. vollständig umbearbeitete Auflage*. Leipzig: Hesse.

——— 1895. "Unsere Konservatorien." In *Präludien und Studien*, vol. 1. Leipzig 1895. Reprinted 1967. Hildesheim: Georg Olms.

——— 1877. *Musikalische Syntaxis: Grundriss einer harmonischen Satzbildungslehre*. Leipzig: Breitkopf.

Robert-Tornow, G. 1907. *Max Reger und Karl Straube*. Göttingen: Otto Hapke.

Schreiber, O. 1956. *Max Reger: Briefe zwischen der Arbeit*. Bonn: Dümmler.

Schreiber, O., and Schreiber, I., eds. 1981a. *Max Reger in seinen Konzerten*, vol. 2. Bonn: Dümmler.

——— eds. 1981b. *Max Reger in seinen Konzerten*, vol. 3. Bonn: Dümmler.

Schweitzer, A. 1906. *Deutsche und Französische Orgelbaukunst und Orgelkunst*. Leipzig: Breitkopf.

Shigihara, S. ed.. 1990. *"Die Konfusion in der Musik": Felix Draesekes Kampfschrift von 1906 und ihre Folgen*. Bonn: Gudrun Schröder.

Sievers, G. 1967. *Die Grundlagen Hugo Riemanns bei Max Reger*. Wiesbaden: Breitkopf.

Slonimsky, N. 1953. *Lexicon of Musical Invective: Critical Assaults on Composers Since Beethoven's Time*. New York: Coleman-Ross Company.

Smolian, A. 1903. Review of Max Reger, *Beiträge zur Modulationslehre*. *Neue Musikalische Presse* 12/21: 377–78.

Straube, K., ed. 1904. *Alte Meister des Orgelspiels: Eine Sammlung deutscher OrgerlKompositionen aus dem XVIII und XVIII Jahrhundert*. Leipzig: C.F. Peters.

Strauss, R. 1907. "Gibt es für die Musik eine Fortschrittspartei?" *Der Morgen* 1/1: 15–18. L. J. Lawrence, trans. 1953. "Is There an Avant-Garde in Music?" In W. Schuh, ed. *Recollections and Reflections*. London: Boosey and Hawkes.

Stravinksy, I. 1942. *Poetics of Music in the Form of Six Lessons*. Trans. A. Knodel and I. Dahl. Cambridge, MA: Harvard University Press.

Taubmann, O. 1903. Review of Max Reger, *Beiträge zur Modulationslehre*. *Neue Zeitschrift für Musik* 70/50: 655.

Wilske, H. 1995. *Max Reger: Zur Rezeption in seiner Zeit*. Wiesbaden: Breitkopf.

Index

N

O

P

Q

R

S

T

U

V

W